SEASIDE GARDENING

PLANTINGS, PROCEDURES, AND DESIGN PRINCIPLES

SUSAN S. H. LITTLEFIELD

Principal Photographer: Derek Fell

Simon and Schuster
New York

A QUARTO BOOK

Published by Simon and Schuster
A Division of Simon & Schuster, Inc.
Simon & Schuster Building
Rockefeller Center
1230 Avenue of the Americas
New York, New York 10020

SIMON AND SCHUSTER and colophon are registered trademarks of Simon & Schuster, Inc.

Library of Congress Cataloging in Publication Data
available upon request.

Paperback edition ISBN 0-671-60242-X • Hardcover edition ISBN 0-671-62222-6

SEASIDE GARDENING: *Plantings, Procedures, and Design Principles*
was prepared and produced by
Quarto Marketing Ltd.
15 West 26th Street
New York, N.Y. 10010

Editor: Mary Forsell
Designer: Judy Goldstein
Photo research: Susan M. Duane, Susan Littlefield
Production Manager: Karen L. Greenberg

Typeset by BPE Graphics, Inc.
Color separations by Hong Kong Scanner Craft Company, Ltd.
Printed and bound in Hong Kong by Leefung-Asco Printers Ltd.

DEDICATION

For my parents, who taught me to love Cape Cod and gardens

ACKNOWLEDGMENTS

With profound thanks to the many gardeners and designers
who have so generously given so much.

CONTENTS

THE SEASIDE ENVIRONMENT

THE ELEMENTS
WIND • WEATHER • SAND • SALT

SEASIDE AREAS
ON THE SEA • BY THE SEA • NEAR THE SEA

FUNDAMENTALS OF SEASIDE DESIGN

DEVELOPING A PLAN
INFORMAL SCHEMES • FORMAL SCHEMES

BALANCING VIEW AND SHELTER
WORKING WITH A VIEW • PROVIDING SHELTER

ELEMENTS OF DESIGN

OUTDOOR ROOMS AND AMENITIES
PORCHES • TERRACES AND DECKS • PERGOLAS • SUMMERHOUSES • GROUNDS FOR GAMES • SWIMMING POOLS • LIGHTING

THE PLANT PALETTE
TREES • SHRUBS • ROSES • HERBACEOUS PLANTS • VINES • GROUND COVERS • LAWNS

COLOR

INTRODUCTION

From Pliny to Pleasure Grounds

A seaside garden begins with the sea—with an open expanse of brilliant blue water and beautiful views, with sparkling light, shifting sands, and bracing salty breezes combining to create conditions entirely pleasant for people though perilous for all but the hardiest plants. Even the swarthy species that do manage to survive by the shore fare best with some protection from the elements; yet protection is hard to come by in coastal gardens. Paradoxically, exposure is the essence of a seaside site, for without it the views, the extraordinary light, and the refreshing winds would be lost. Thus, gardening by the sea is a particularly challenging endeavor, for the goal is to create a place that is both open and enclosed, providing pleasurable grounds for plants and people.

With that fundamental aim in mind, virtually anything goes. Formal and informal, practical and exotic—all themes are part of the seaside tradition. Some coastal gardens are precisely structured with clipped hedges and topiary, others are arranged so casually that they seem to be part of the existing scenery. One will be filled with flowers, an-

A corner of Reef Point, Beatrix Farrand's garden in Bar Harbor, Maine.

other will be accentuated with a single specimen tree. Some seaside gardens are fanciful in spirit, reflecting the pleasurable associations of sun, surf, and summer holidays; others soberly embrace the austerity of the coastal landscape, incorporating only those materials that would occur naturally. Each approach has merit, in the right place and with the right person controlling the design. Style, in gardening, art, architecture, and fashion, has always been a matter of personal taste.

The Beginnings

One of the first seaside gardeners on record is Pliny the Younger. His villa, perched on the Italian coast at Laurentinum, was probably typical of the seaside retreats favored by Romans seeking to escape the heat of the city summers. According to reconstructions, the villa was a classical combination of buildings, pergolas, and terraces, with its walls lapped by wind and waves. A room for summer dining stretched out into the sea; for winter, a second dining room was set in a more sheltered section of the villa. Pliny wrote of using rosemary plants to border flower beds with their fragrant perfumes, as his boxwood suffered in the salt spray; he also cultivated violets, figs, and mulberry trees.

Pliny's less wealthy peers tended far simpler gardens, no doubt; unfortunately, however, few of their efforts remain. The early gardens that were documented were oasislike paradises set in the

Grasses and ground covers are encouraged to naturalize on a rocky slope in the British Isles, with surprisingly rich results.

middle of barren landscapes (a situation that usually resulted in a four-square plan surrounded by walls) or terraced gardens like the ones chiseled out of the hills around Rome.

It is safe to assume that many of the gardens by the sea were far less splendid. Some of the earliest seaside gardeners had to have been the wives of the fishermen, merchants, and seafaring men who lived in coastal villages. Their cottage plots would have been practical places where fruits, vegetables, and flowers found comfortable footing between chicken coops and compost piles. That tradition survives in coastal towns like Nantucket and Annapolis, where window boxes are brimming with flowers and dooryard gardens overflow with carefully nurtured crops of herbs or lettuces grown alongside roses, hollyhocks, and hostas set in the shade of a small fruit tree.

Mounds of low-growing plants on a massive outcrop in Prince and Princess Nicholas Abkhazi's garden in British Columbia.

The Practical Pioneers

The adventurers who settled the shores of the New World were more intent on farming than gardening, for they had to oversee the cultivation of the food crops that were essential to the survival of their colonies. In the early seventeenth century, Champlain complained that fields planted on an island off of the Maine coast were not nearly as fruitful as mainland plots; but Captain John Smith reported success with a crop of "green sallets" grown in an island garden nearby. In Boston harbor, Governor Winthrop's garden was a productive model, complete with an apple orchard and a vineyard.

By the end of the seventeenth century, urbane settlers of port towns were beginning to favor more decorative gardens. Maps of Manhattan show houses surrounded by formally patterned beds. Further south, travelers described roses blooming in the streets of the settlement at St. Augustine, Florida.

A dazzling display of annuals carpets a garden in Eastbourne, along the English coast and adds to the festive air of the waterfront.

European Palaces and Pleasure Grounds

New World settlers and generations of gardeners since have been inspired by England—for gardens grow luxuriantly in the mild climate of the British Isles, and their cultivation combines a national passion with a fine artistic tradition. The English set seaside gardening on a new course in the eighteenth century, with the discovery of natural springs in the coastal town of Southampton. Springs had inspired the development of spas elsewhere in England, but a combination of tradition and superstition had worked against the creation of seaside resorts. Salt water was considered unhealthy, and those dauntless enough to bathe in it were subject to taxation, for the sea was part of the king's domain. A Spa House was opened at Southampton in 1700 (nearly eighty years after the spring's discovery), but the seaside did not become a popular recreational resort until the late eighteenth century when an English doctor launched a campaign promoting the healthy benefits of salt water.

Seaside villas developed around the spas—the most noteworthy, by far, being the Royal Pavilion at Brighton. A fanciful recreation of an Indian palace, Brighton inspired a flurry of seaside architectural follies. Exoticism was the rage in horticulture as in

Esteban and Harriet Vicente's Long Island garden is a cottage-inspired combination of flowers.

Historical Museum of Southern Florida

Florida's Gold Coast was developed in the early 1900s with lavish hotels set in lushly landscaped grounds.

Twentieth-Century Amusements

The American public also enjoyed seaside pleasures. People flocked to Atlantic City's boardwalks and Coney Island's amusements by the millions in the early 1900s. Brooklyn's Coney Island was a sandspit in the 1880s, but within twenty years, the native scrub vegetation had been replaced by acres of sidewalks, rides, hotdog stands, and exotic plants. Seventy thousand new palms and plants were hauled in annually for the opening of Luna Park's new season. Although display gardens took second place to the more active offerings of the American amusement parks, they were definitely part of the picture.

architecture, and estate gardeners sprinkled their picturesquely landscaped grounds with Italianate terraces, French parterres, Persian pools, and Chinese temples.

Next came the railroad, and with it, hordes of people escaping the heat and monotony of city summers. Hotels and resorts sprang up along the coast, each surrounded by lavishly landscaped gardens. Glass houses called winter gardens provided lush quarters for tropical plants; exotic display gardens complete with rockeries, waterfalls, and elaborately patterned beds of seasonal flowers were planted along waterfront promenades connected by networks of tree-lined paths. Cliff walks were created wherever the natural terrain allowed, affording a pleasant place to walk and survey the scenery. These were so popular that the resorts with attractive waterfront walks prospered without ornamental gardens, according to architectural historian Kenneth Lindley in his book *Seaside Architecture*. Sites that were not endowed with spectacular places to promenade tended to develop elaborate gardens instead. Variations aside, the seaside was clearly a place for pleasure for nineteenth-century Englishmen, and gardens were one of the prime attractions.

A series of twisted stone steps winds down a cliff to the beach in Robert Stigwood's Bermuda garden.

Changing Tastes

Back in the garden—English ones, most notably—the tide turned toward the end of the nineteenth century, as writers and gardeners like William Robinson and Gertrude Jekyll advocated a more natural style of growing plants. "Where things are well, let well alone," was their advice, and they practiced their principles in the grounds around their country houses. Although neither Robinson nor Jekyll lived near the shore, the ideas that they generated changed the way gardeners in England and elsewhere thought about their plans and planting. The tender plants and highly decorative bedding schemes that gave so many seaside resorts their sparkle were among Robinson's prime targets: In his many books and articles, he insisted on the use of species plants and wildflowers that were hardy enough to survive in permanent beds. Jekyll expressed her disdain for formal bedding schemes most eloquently in her gardens, where mixed drifts of plants were loosely arranged according to height and color.

Miss Jekyll is universally admired for her contribution to the art of flower gardening; and because

Bouganvillea bounds over a gate in a village garden in the Bahamas.

flowers are so successful by the sea, her influence on seaside gardens has been considerable. Her effect extends far beyond the herbaceous border, however. "I am strongly for treating garden and wooded ground in a pictorial way, . . . and for so arranging plants and trees and grassy spaces that they look happy and at home, and make no parade of conscious effort," she wrote in *Wood and Garden*. In creating pleasing pictures, Jekyll paid particularly keen attention to the edges of her gardens—the places where cultivated flowers gradually gave way to native trees and shrubs. Her perimeter plantings provide invaluable inspiration for seaside gardeners, for they ensure a smooth transition from the garden to the surrounding landscape. That transition is critical to the success of any composition in which the distant view is as important as the foreground scenery.

The garden at the Breakers in Newport, Rhode Island serves as a setting for the building and the sea.

Modern Trends

Building on foundations laid by the English landscape school and gardeners like Robinson and Jekyll, twentieth-century American designers looked at the landscape with new eyes. Frank Lloyd Wright demonstrated his sensitivity to the land by binding his buildings to their sites with native materials and long, low-slung lines suited to the local topography. Jens Jensen launched a vernacular American style in the Midwestern landscapes that he designed, using a palette of native plants and a subtle technique of interweaving groves and open glades that was inspired by patterns in the indigenous prairie landscape. Today, A. E. Bye practices with a similar philosophy, designing landscapes

Flower beds set in an emerald lawn in front of Golden Gate Park's Conservatory. Extensive engineering transformed San Francisco's sand dunes to the English-style park in the 1870s.

The National Museum of American Art, Smithsonian Institution. Gift of John Gellatly.

Celia Thaxter in her Garden, *painted by Childe Hassam in 1892.*

both on the coast and inland that are virtually impossible to distinguish from their native surroundings.

The trend toward naturalized landscapes has been boosted by ecological and energy issues, as increased awareness has made gardeners sensitive to the futility of cultivating exotic plants in inhospitable surroundings. Rather than depending on windbreaks and protective walls to shelter tender plants, some contemporary gardeners have opted to revise their thinking. They have opened their arms to the sea and reduced their gardens to the plants that will survive in seaside conditions. Theirs is certainly the most practical approach—and, according to some twentieth-century tastes, the most appealing one as well.

CHAPTER ONE

THE SEASIDE ENVIRONMENT

THE ELEMENTS

The rocky outcrops, pounding surf, and windblown salt spray characteristic of the shore are hospitable only to a select group of swarthy plants.

The problems that seaside gardeners have to contend with are primarily the result of wind, sand, and salt; conditions that combine to create an extremely dry environment for growing plants—a desert, in effect. These elements play a major role in determining the design of seaside gardens, for coping with them is far easier than trying to change them. The most effective way to begin a garden by the sea, therefore, is to understand the natural conditions. In the words of one seasoned gardener, Alice Lounsberry, "To acknowledge the difficulties in a seaside garden is, in a measure, to have overcome them." Not every coastal condition is difficult, by any means; but whether an asset or a drawback, each has implications in terms of designing and maintaining a garden.

Wind

Wind is one of the most destructive elements by the shore, for a coastal landscape is exposed both by nature and design. The environment is naturally open because constant winds and shifting sands discourage growth and uproot even the most determined seaside plants. And developed land is likely to be kept partially open as well, in order to take the best advantage of views.

Exposure to wind goes hand in hand with gardening by the shore, therefore, and wind is a double-edged sword, bringing sand and salt as well as gale-force gusts. Wind alone can batter leaves and

break branches, opening a door to disease, and sharp blasts can uproot entire plants and scour away their growing medium. Wind also creates the dramatic silhouettes that are so characteristic of woody shoreline plants. Their sculpted look is not the result of strong or constant winds: It is caused by cold spring winds nipping the tender buds on the windward side of the plant. The result is an uneven shape, which is exaggerated in poor soil, creating dwarfed, densely branched plants with cragged lines. Many alpines and dwarf shrubs—conifers, in particular—are naturally endowed with this rugged, windblown character, and thus are fitting subjects for an exposed seaside site. Wind affects blooming habits as well, for flowers unfold most successfully, and in far greater numbers, on the lee sides of seaside plants.

Onshore breezes are laden with salt, and as they blow well beyond the beach, they extend the seaside zone considerably inland. Gardens set several blocks from the beach are subject to significantly high concentrations of airborne salt; even places several miles from the shore are vulnerable to occasional baths in salt spray. Spring storms are the most destructive, churning up seawater that burns the tender new leaves of all but the thickest-skinned seaside plants. Airborne salt is also a factor to be reckoned with in selecting material to grow near the shore: Although barely evident to gardeners, it is noxious to many plants. In peripheral seaside zones, for instance, Norway maples (*Acer platanoides*) fare better than sugar or silver maples (*A. saccarinum, A. tomentosum*) because their coarse leaves are impervious to airborne salt. The bracing sea air is not all bad, by any means. Many seaside gardeners claim that salt serves as an antiseptic, helping to ward off the fungal diseases that thrive in the moist sea air.

Wind-borne sand is also a nuisance to plants and plantsmen. In small amounts it is abrasive, breaking down bark and protective leaf surfaces; in substantial quantities it can be altogether destructive, either burying or uprooting entire plants. Sandblasting does far more damage in seaside gardens than salt spray does, according to Edwin A. Menninger, author of *Seaside Plants of the World*. His book, incidentally, is a far more comprehensive guide to gardening than its title suggests, and should be on every serious seaside gardener's reading list.

Dessication is perhaps the most persistent problem caused by coastal winds, for even the mildest breezes become more intense with the sand's reflected heat and parch plants in their paths. All seaside plants need protection from this drying heat; some are specially adapted with small leaves or deep roots (see chapter 4 "Selecting Seaside Plants"), others are dependent upon the shelter provided by geography and pioneer vegetation.

A path at Exbury Gardens lined with rhododendrons and azaleas. Many rare species have been developed at Exbury, encouraged, no doubt, by the mild, moist climate of southern England.

Along the California coast, twisted bare trunks of native pines and cypresses have been blasted by constant wind and are stunted by the lack of nutrients available in the sandy soil.

Weather

Climatic conditions vary around the world, yet coastal communities share a number of similarities in their weather. Clear days are extraordinarily bright, as light comes from almost every direction—reflected by sand, water, and an unobstructed sky. The resulting heat is intense, particularly when combined with the drying winds, and the glare can be relentless. These effects are amplified by the limited vegetative cover, which exaggerates the open topography and contributes little in the way of shady relief.

Although the hot sun wreaks havoc with plants, seaside light has long been an inspiration to gardeners. Something about watery light is magic—its shimmering quality, perhaps, or the endless changes in its intensity and the way this is reflected in the water's surface. The light seems soft in the moist air and, as the work of the Impressionists and other landscape painters documents, it has a wonderful effect on colors. Even the simplest flowers seem more luxuriantly brilliant by the sea than in the most lavish inland gardens, as generations of artists, writers, and seaside gardeners have attested.

Luxuriant growth is due, in part, to the temperate nature of coastal climates. Water changes temperature far more slowly than land, and it modulates weather dramatically as a result. Seasons are out-of-sync by the shore: Spring and summer tend to be cool, fall is usually warm, and the first frost comes to the seaside several weeks later than to nearby landlocked places.

Blooming sequences are topsy-turvy, too. "Sometimes it is as if the order of nature were set aside in this spot," wrote nineteenth-century artist Celia Thaxter in her book *An Island Garden* describing her garden on Appledore Island off the Maine coast, "for you find the eyebright and pimpernel and white violets growing side by side until the frost comes in November; often October passes with no sign of frost,

*Opposite page: A lone palm grows in a garden in Inverewe, Scotland, where the climate is modulated by the warm waters of the Gulf Stream. **Above:** American beach grass is one of the first plants to grow above the high water line. **Below left:** Evergreen shrubs hug the foundation of a Massachusetts summerhouse acting as barriers against the elements and providing attractive year round foliage as well. **Below right:** Pines and a dusky gray-green ground cover called poverty grass are the only plants that grow in the hollows of these East coast dunes.*

ing effect of water nearby. Tender plants appreciate a wind screen of burlap wrap, however, to protect them from potentially fatal blasts of cold winter air.

The shore's delayed spring affects planting plans as well, for it means that annuals are slow in getting started. Some seasoned gardeners feel that annuals are all too frustrating in coastal beds, for they reach their peak just as frost comes. Perennials and bulbs are valuable, particularly in the first weeks of spring, for they leaf out early and are hardy enough to stand up to an occasional late-season cold snap.

Sand

Sandy soil is typical along the shore, and it presents both problems and benefits. Sand is grainy, with pockets of air between the particles that warm up quickly, contributing to the wind's drying effect. But more important, water percolates quickly through sand. It is lost almost immediately, in fact: On the surface, it evaporates in the dry heat, and once in the ground, it drains quickly and thoroughly, because sand includes very little of the spongy organic material that soaks moisture up. The sparse supply of organic matter also means that sandy soil holds few nutrients; if the soil consists of a great many ground-up shells, the situation is even worse. Shells are made of calcium—lime in gardening terms—and in massive doses, lime locks up the few available nutrients, thereby preventing their absorption by plants.

To improve moisture retention and enhance the supply of nutrients, sandy soil needs to be supplemented with organic material. Topsoil is organic, but as it is heavy, it tends to sink between the lighter grains of sand. Peat moss, ground bark, leaf mold, and manure help create humus, a soft organic material well-suited to filling in the open pores that are typical of sandy soil. A compost heap is a boon to any seaside garden, as a result, for it converts

and the autumn lingers longer than elsewhere. I have seen the iris and wild-rose and goldenrod and aster in blossom together, as if, not having the example of the world before their eyes, they followed their own sweet will, and blossomed when they took the fancy.''

Daniel J. Foley, author of *Gardening by the Sea*, summarized the seaside influence somewhat more systematically. ''The sea is a great leveler,'' he wrote, referring most particularly to the plants that grow within

its reach. Species of borderline hardiness often thrive by the shore, despite the categories assigned by seasoned horticulturists, for the seaside is a microclimate—mild enough to qualify as a separate, more temperate zone. Camellias grow on Cape Cod, combining a species of plant hardy to Zone 7 and a place that is typically rated as Zone 6 (see page 81); jacarandas shiver through New York winters; palms grow in Ireland; and kiwi fruit burgeon as far north as Oregon, thanks to the warm-

weeds and household scraps into a constant supply of rich, humusy mulch.

Sandy soil, like salty air, is not entirely bad. It is far easier to garden in than heavy clay soil, for instance. Even rapid drainage can be considered an asset, because very few plants can tolerate standing in water-logged soil. Since it contains so little standing water, sandy soil does not freeze readily: It is workable for a long season and subject to less heaving than heavier soils, which means less winter damage to permanent plantings.

Salt

Salt holds water, and thererfore it competes with plants, for water held by salt is not available to roots or any of the other plant tissues. In the air, salt burns sensitive leaves; in the soil, it competes for available moisture; and in the water, it is toxic to the tissues of all but the most specialized plants. Seawater is 2½ percent salt: A solution with only 1½ percent salt is fatal to the leaves, stems, and roots of most ordinary plants. Salt, in sum, is not good for plants. Being so attracted to water, however, salt is easily washed away. Fresh water thus proves to be one of the keys to a salt-resistant garden. Periodic rinsings are the surest way to success with plants that are subject to salt either above or below the soil surface.

Salt tends to accumulate in sandy soils, for it is left behind as the moisture in the ground evaporates and percolates. Here again, Mr. Foley's description of the effect is apt: "It would seem that the presence of salt builds up a thirst in plants as it does in humans," he writes, "causing them to root deeply in search of water and to store it as protection against drought." Given salt's affinity for water, however, its concentration in the soil tends to exaggerate the effect of drought. Although the addition of spongy organic material does enhance the soil's capacity to retain moisture, it does not eliminate the problem of salt buildup: Basically, more water also means more salt. Periodic deep soakings—or leachings—are the most effective solution for garden soils that are laden with salt. Prevention is a far better cure, however, and it is possible with good drainage and systematic watering. A consistent schedule of generous soakings will ensure that fresh water is constantly leaching through the soil and removing the excess salt.

Rinsing is the best antidote to saltwater flooding. Lawns subjected to saline soakings can be treated with ground limestone and a fresh-water bath, once all traces of

Above: *A meadow in Point Lobos, California is a richly detailed tapestry of low-growing plants that tolerate wind and salt.* **Right:** *Stacks of weathered lobster pots, evergreens, and fog are typical of northern New England's coastal landscapes.*

A wooden deck, a lawn, and a rugged stepping stone path that weaves between mounds of silver-leaved plants provide a boldly uncomplicated landscape for a house in southern California that opens onto the Pacific ocean. Isabelle C. Greene & Associates, landscape architects.

standing salt water are gone. When applying limestone, the ratio should be twenty to fifty pounds per one thousand square feet, and the watering should be thorough. Salt water is least destructive when the ground is already damp, and thus a good soaking is desirable preparation for a storm that is likely to cause saltwater floods. Leaves and branches that have been drenched in salty water will benefit from a vigorous and thorough rinsing as soon after the storm as possible.

Salt is not anathema to all plants, however. Small concentrations of salt in the soil encourage some plants to develop lush, healthy root systems. Halophytes are the plants that survive in extremely salty soils, and they tend to be succulent, with ample supplies of soft, water-filled tissue. Although few gardeners have such salty conditions that they must rely on true halophytes, succulence can be a clue in the search for salt-tolerant plants. Turnips and potatoes are two root vegetables that thrive in slightly salty soils, for instance; cabbages, brussels sprouts, pumpkins, and globe artichokes also seem to take well to seaside situations—most notably in the foggy, windswept fields that line the coasts of California and Long Island.

SEASIDE AREAS

Opposite page: Ancient trees tower above the lawn at Exbury Gardens, shading rhododendrons and azaleas. Above left: Porches are the primary feature of oceanfront yards on Martha's Vineyard. Above right: Steep stairways and tenacious plants cling to California bluffs.

Seaside gardens vary in situation just as they vary in style. Some sit low on the water's edge, lapped by waves and salt spray; others are perched high on bluffs; some border salt marshes, and others are several miles from the water's edge, with no apparent relationship to the ocean. One of the simplest ways to define a seaside situation is to include any site that is exposed to winds carrying sand and salt, but that can be misleading, for some gardens that seem protected are subject to seaside conditions. In the interest of being more specific, this book will focus on three different seaside areas.

On the Sea

The most obvious seaside garden is set right on the beach. If it qualifies as a garden, it is probably not in the dunes just behind the beach, where only beach grass and a few pioneer plants can survive in the shifting sands; more likely, it will be set back a bit. Though this landscape also is open and exposed, the growing conditions are a bit more favorable, and a greater number of plants are able to survive here. Beach grasses and tough her-baceous plants trap the sand, providing a somewhat solid footing for pioneer species of shrubs like beach plum, bayberry, and salt spray rose.

The simplest garden for this area—sometimes referred to as the secondary dune—is a naturalized one, with native plants grouped in loose clumps or hummocks. A thick cover of beach grass helps hold sand in place; shrubs bring flowers, attract birds, and add height and texture; and evergreen trees that can stand up to ocean winds and salt spray provide protection for the places and plants in their lee. As an example, A.E. Bye's Long Island landscape is a naturalized garden, planted to protect a man-made dune and to provide privacy for a newly constructed house. It consists of only five species of plants, but they were used in massive quantities so as to resemble the broad sweeps of plants that occur naturally.

Whereas a naturalized garden includes the plants most appropriate to the environment, a more conventional garden tends to modify the conditions to suit less well-adapted plants. Protection is the key to establishing exotic plants on the secondary dune, and it is essential to the creation of a more cultivated garden. A wooden fence can shelter a small patch of flowers; for a larger garden, a combination of mounded earth and a windbreak of densely planted trees and shrubs is a more effective solution.

Carpobrotus blankets Pacific slopes.

By the Sea

A second type of seaside garden sits by the water in a somewhat more protected situation. Both horizontal and vertical distance mitigate the effect of the wind and waves; thus a garden set back from the beach or raised on a bluff high above the surf can provide a comfortable niche for plants that could not survive closer to the water. A narrow neck of land or an offshore island can also shelter a waterfront garden. In such places, the conditions differ from those on the secondary dune only in degree. The wind is generally a bit weaker, carrying less sand and salt, and the native vegetation is more varied. Perhaps the most significant change is in the soil. The increased cover has introduced a new source of organic material that enriches the soil.

Masses of ice plants have naturalized along the California coast. The fleshy leaves store moisture, encouraging survival in sand; and they multiply quickly, protecting and anchoring the dunes.

A meadow full of lupine is a bold foreground for a harbor view in Maine.

Beds of brightly colored annuals bloom just a block from the ocean on Long Island. A hedge protects flowers from wind and sets the beds apart from the coarse grasses nearby.

Primulas and bluebells blooming in the dappled shade of cutleaf Japanese maples in a naturalized corner of the grounds at Exbury, a garden set on an estuary in southern England.

Mackenzie Bell's backyard garden in Brighton features plants that tolerate salt air.

A stand of gnarled trees defines the edge of a Long Island lawn, marking the transition from the green, level garden to the undulating topography and shrubby native plants of the dunes.

Near the Sea

Some seaside gardens are not literally by the sea but are subjected to seaside conditions nonetheless. A piece of land that abuts a marsh or a tidal creek is likely to have sandy soil and salt, either in the air or in the groundwater; if the view is kept open, it will be exposed to wind as well. Some inland gardens also have a decidedly seaside influence: Although the water may seem miles away, it tempers the local climate. Backyard gardens in the middle of San Francisco and Los Angeles, for instance, are wrapped in fog for a good part of the growing season—a condition that influences the selection and cultivation of plants.

CHAPTER TWO

FUNDAMENTALS OF SEASIDE DESIGN

DEVELOPING A PLAN

Gardens by the sea include central open spaces that allow for views, with enclosing elements added, as necessary, to create protected places for plants and people. Windbreaks and screens are the garden's exterior walls; hedges, fences, low walls, and mounds of raised earth divide the space within into a series of separate rooms. Garden rooms range from architectonic to picturesque, depending on the character and configuration of the enclosing elements. Whether formal or informal, the more effective the enclosure, the more extensive and exotic the plan and plantings within.

Opposite page: A rock outcrop and view. *Leonore Baronio, landscape designer.* **Above:** *A hedge defines the water's edge. Edward D. Stone & Associates, landscape architects.*

Informal Schemes

In the most exposed seaside situations, an informal approach is almost essential, for only the hardiest native plants grouped in dense masses will survive the salt spray and constant wind. Elsewhere, informality is a matter of choice; most logically, perhaps, where an informal or naturalistic plan fits most harmoniously into the surrounding scenery. Informal schemes have an instinctive appeal as well. And, for reasons that range from ecological to aesthetic, they are an increasingly appropriate choice for contemporary gardeners. If well planned, they require minimal maintenance and they suit twentieth-century tastes for casual, carefree style.

The indigenous seaside landscape is the model for the most naturalistic coastal gardens, with masses of plants distributed in irregular groups consisting of various sizes and species. Dusty-miller, beach grass, ice plant, and other low herbaceous plants grow along beachfronts; shrubby species like bayberry, beach plum, sea grape, or yaupon holly cluster in mounds between the dunes. Red cedars and pines, palms and scrub oaks associate further inland, where more stable conditions encourage the growth and maturation of larger plants. Transitions between the different areas are smooth, and within each one the plant associations are consistent. The seaside landscape has remarkable unity as a result—and that is the quality that informal plans strive to capture.

Following nature's example does not mean leaving the design to chance, however. Creating a natural-looking garden can involve every bit as much artistry as laying out a formal one, in fact. Spaces are defined by irregular masses of mixed plants; clearings are carefully structured to allow for views and privacy. Individual

A border with ground covers, annuals, and perennials lines the perimeter of a waterfront yard in Maine providing color and an ample supply of flowers for cutting without restricting the view of Boothbay Harbor. The weathered rock is a becoming background for blossoms and silvery leaves.

features are planned to provide interest without distracting from the harmony of the larger landscape. Success comes with a unified scheme that is balanced and well-composed without looking overworked—or without looking worked at all, for that matter. Appearances aside, an informal plan that fits comfortably into the surrounding scenery can be exceptionally difficult to design.

In planting as in planning, informal gardens are not always as natural as they appear to be. The English landscape

school has inspired countless numbers of picturesquely informal gardens that include exotic plants and materials arranged with minimal attention to the patterns and associations of the local ecology. Thus, informal seaside gardens are essentially like informal inland gardens: They consist of curves, mixed plantings, and stretches of lawn that highlight the clean silhouettes of specimen trees. The seaside garden's distinction lies primarily in the selection of appropriate plants and the treatment of the site's periphery, where the informal

merges with the indigenous coastal landscape. The transition should be subtle in informal schemes, with the garden's regular lines and exotic materials gradually giving way to local patterns and plants.

In a naturalized scheme, the existing landscape is edited rather than rearranged. Space might be cleared for views and an occasional exotic plant introduced to spice the native palette, but, ultimately, a successful naturalized garden is so informal that it is barely discernible from the landscape that surrounds it.

Formal Schemes

A formal plan begins with enclosure and crisp lines that separate the garden from the native landscape. Perimeter walls, fences, and hedges introduce the geometric structure that is fundamental to formality, and they also provide shelter—which is essential to any seaside scheme that hopes to achieve a consistently formal effect. Exotic plants like boxwood and yew, tender annuals, and roses are traditionally incorporated in formal plans—and for good reason. They are a dependable group: The evergreens give year-round color and form, and their finely textured foliage creates an appropriately subdued backdrop for the annuals' brilliant display. Roses, lilies, spring-flowering bulbs, and any other short-seasoned bloomers are most effective when formally displayed because the patterns of hedges, paths, and grassy parterres provide order once the blossoms have faded. Some seaside gardeners have achieved spectacular effects with less conventional materials, incidentally. At Vizcaya—a subtropical Italianate garden set on the edge of Miami's Biscayne Bay—the parterre is structured with lines of clipped podocarpus, and the walls are softened by masses of plumbago and bougainvillea. Walls structure the most classic formal plans, providing an architectural framework that offsets the garden's greenery. In terms of plant material, some of the best formal gardens are green, although a formal plan can be a spectacular setting for flowers.

Paths are the seams that bind the garden's different parts together, escorting and orienting people through an unfolding display, and their development is fundamental to the style and success of the design. Paths typically mark the axes in formal schemes, and offset patterned beds with uniform lines of stone, gravel, or grass. They wander less directly in naturalized gardens, conforming to irregularities in the topography and weaving around the uneven masses of mixed groups of trees and shrubs.

Boardwalks are the classic seaside paths: They keep feet on a single track, thereby reducing wear and tear to fragile dunes, and being elevated, they provide a protected niche for plants. Beach grasses, herbaceous plants, and shrubs can find comfortable footing under and alongside raised paths, where the risk of being trampled by clumsy feet is minimal. Wooden walkways are among the easiest to build in sandy soils. They are also the least intrusive—both visually and ecologically—for wood weathers to a soft silvery patina that suits a landscape washed by wind and water. Boardwalks can be raised high above the level of the sand to provide views. But if the view of the path is more dramatic than the view from it, sunken walkways are a better solution. These are effective only in stable soils, however; in exposed situations, a sunken path is likely to erode or be buried in a barrage of windblown sand.

An axis defined by topiary shrubs, steps, and a low-lying pool points to the water. Distant trees disrupt the linear scheme, creating privacy and an appealing sense of mystery.

BALANCING VIEW AND SHELTER

A garden that sits by the sea is designed like a three-sided room, typically taking full advantage of its waterfront situation by opening out to an expansive view. Exposure goes hand in hand with views, however: The fourth side of the garden "room" serves as a window, but is actually a door to wind, sand, and salt spray. Plants need protection from such potentially destructive elements, if they are to thrive, and providing that protection without sacrificing the open view is the fundamental challenge in gardening by the sea.

Nature provides the open view, with stunning dunes and rocky shores. But since these seaside elements are not particularly hospitable to plants, providing shelter is the gardener's job. Shelter is the essence of garden-making, in fact: It sets gardens apart from natural landscapes, defining them as special places for selected plants. Thus gardeners are naturally biased—or at least the best ones are, in the opinion of Alice Martineau, an early-twentieth-century garden connoisseur and the author of *Gardening in Sunny Lands: The Riviera, California, Australia.* There she states that "...he who lives in and for his garden, and makes his plants his first consideration, may have to sacrifice the dream of a sheltered garden combined with a far-reaching view, and be content with a site protected from cold winds, but therefore necessarily less open."

In addition to horticultural and aesthetic considerations, the realities of seaside real estate often play a significant role in determining garden plans. Waterfront lots are small and narrow, typically—a pattern that puts privacy at a premium. So where development is dense, seaside gardeners are apt to favor enclosure, setting up fences or hedgerows as protective screens along their property lines.

Sculpture in a small, protected parterre. Innocenti & Webel, landscape architects.

Working with a View

Whether expansive or narrow, a water view is a dominant design element. Water is a notable eye-catcher: A glimpse of water miles in the distance commands attention far disproportionate to the amount of the space it occupies in the view. Whatever the size, distant water manages to subjugate elements in the foreground, thereby contributing to the effect of a unified landscape scene. A garden on the water, therefore, should be planned as part of a picture, for it serves not only as a place, but also as a setting for the view. The best plans are simple, designed to complement rather than compete with the surrounding scenery. Scale is far more important to the success of a seaside garden than its style: Generous

A formal flower garden framed by a protective hedge that opens to reveal a water view.

Terraces created by railroad-tie retaining walls step down to a sheltered spot for sitting. Waist-high beds bring flowers and herbs within easy reach and are scaled to suit the site.

terrace edge give a comfortable sense of enclosure, for example, although the protection actually provided is minimal. A single specimen tree set to one side of the view can also contribute to the creation of a sense of place in a seaside garden.

When protection is essential, the necessary hedges or walls should frame the view without competing with the scenery beyond. The edge between the garden and the seaside landscape is particularly critical, in visual terms: In front of a significant view, it should be unobtrusive, so as to ensure a smooth transition from the foreground to the distant scenery. The cultivated garden's rich palette of plants should be replaced by a simpler selection of native species toward the shore; finely textured plants and cool-colored leaves that enhance atmospheric perspective are more appropriate than bold foliage and bright flowers. A hard line cutting across a view is jarring: Where unavoidable, seaside gardeners would do well to heed Humphrey Repton's advice by planting informally on both sides of the line.

proportions should grace both formal and informal schemes, as fussy features and intricate details are awkward incidentals when seen in front of a panoramic view.

Not every water view is naturally picture-perfect, however. A lengthy view channeled through a narrow lot can be constrictive, with the sides more dominant than the distant sea, and an expansive view can be breathtaking but unremittingly boring at second glance. Water itself is rarely dull, for it changes constantly with the play of wind and light. An entirely open ocean view, however, can be overwhelming, particularly in the face of relentless winds and glaring light.

Establishing the Foreground

As landscape painters know, a view is enhanced by a foreground that establishes a sense of scale, and by a frame that provides definition. A stand of lacy-leaved trees set to the side of a water view can provide welcome relief and structure, for instance: The trunks offset the stark, flat line of the distant horizon, the branches create a comforting scale, and the leaves provide shade. A pergola or summerhouse could have similar value in a more formal scheme. No matter what the style of the surrounding garden, a subtle screen makes an open view infinitely more appealing. Mystery piques curiosity, and a glimpse gives even the most complacent onlooker incentive to explore further.

The larger challenge is to maintain an open view while providing some enclosure. Where the sense of exposure is more psychological than physical, merely suggesting shelter can be an effective solution. Scale is more important than protection in this instance, as any feature that establishes human proportion in the landscape will be a source of comfort, visually. A low wall or a line of flowers along a

Celia Thaxter's enclosed cutting garden.

Providing Shelter

Providing shelter is a building process, entirely different from clearing, which opens views. Buffering winds, screening unpleasant sights, and creating cool shade are structural goals, and as they are achieved, the garden takes the shape of an alfresco house, with a series of outdoor rooms enclosed by protective walls.

Whether the plan is formal or informal, protection begins at the garden's periphery. Native species mark the first line of defense, bearing the brunt of the wind and salt spray and shielding masses of less-hardy plants in their lee. Hedges and low walls provide more orderly protection, and many shrubs and herbaceous perennials prosper behind them. Houses and out-buildings also shelter plants: The spaces that they create are suitable for the most intensively cultivated gardens where leaves and fragile flowers can unfold without the risk of being battered by gusty winds, and tender plants can bask in the heat and light reflected by the surrounding walls.

Above left: Walls shelter a garden on the Texas coast. Ford, Powell & Carson, landscape architects. *Above right:* A roof frames a Pacific view. Isabelle C. Greene, landscape architect. *Below:* Fence and breakwater are artfully combined. Engel/GGP, landscape architects.

Breaking the Wind

Breaking the wind is the first step in sheltering a seaside garden. Although prevailing winds are important to consider, they actually account for less than half of the breezes that blow on oceanfront gardens. Storm winds do the most extensive damage, and they can come from any quadrant. The cautious planner anticipates the worst possible weather, and is not overly protective of plants. This is because those plants that have been extremely sheltered are most vulnerable when storm winds blow.

Buffering, not blocking, is the best way to break wind. A solid windblock creates destructively turbulent eddies, and if built of anything less sturdy than stone, the barrier itself will be subject to occasional wind damage. Wind screens are best for buffering. The most effective of these has a surface ratio of 40 percent penetrable to 60 percent inpenetrable. Height is also important: A screen of 40:60 density creates a protected area seven or eight times its height on the lee side. The wind's speed will be reduced for a distance of approximately twenty times the barrier's height.

Shelterbelts and Hedges

A shelterbelt is a living fence planted with tough, reliable trees and shrubs. The dense undergrowth buffers wind, creating a snug harbor for tender low-growing plants, and the wispy treetops sift breezes without causing turbulent eddies. The result is an efficient windbreak, particularly when composed of indigenous species.

For this reason, shelterbelts are often planted to protect waterfront gardens. Evergreens make a dependable backbone, for they are full year-round, but species that tend to drop their lower branches need to be underplanted if they are to prove effective in mitigating wind. Dense masses of deciduous trees and shrubs make up the bulk of shelterbelts, with natives and fast-growing pioneer plants providing initial protection for the slower-growing species that will eventually fill in the line.

Hedges are garden walls built with plants, and they range in formality from loose lines of assorted shrubs to meticulously sheared rows of finely textured privet or box. The best hedges are flared at the base so that sun can reach the lower boughs and keep them full and healthy. A tapered profile is also the most efficient windbreak, for it manages to condense the advantages of a shelterbelt into a single plant, buffering breezes at the base and filtering them through the thinner branches on top.

Fences and Walls

A garden wall built of stone or brick blocks the wind and captures the warmth of the sun as well, giving an extra boost to the plants that it protects. The higher the wall, the more protection it provides. But a towering masonry structure is an imposing element by the shore, where the landscape tends to be open and views are desirable. Low walls, however, provide protection for low-growing plants with minimal interruption of the natural terrain.

Walls are by far the most efficient means of creating shelter, for masonry provides maximum protection in minimum spaces. "Why use twenty feet of planting," asks landscape architect Richard Webel, "when you can do the same thing with an eight-inch wall?" His firm, Innocenti & Webel, has used walls to shelter seaside gardens from Maine to Florida.

Any wall that holds earth in place is a retaining wall. Retaining walls are invaluable along sandy shores, for they provide solid footing for plants. Walls that retain sand also help keep beaches from encroaching upon gardens. And, when their beds are enriched with organic material, they serve as overscaled container gardens hospitable to plants that could not survive in ordinary seaside soil.

Stone is a sturdy material for garden walls, but it can look out-of-place along sandy shores. Stone construction is most appropriate in rocky terrain. Ideally, any new stonework will echo the color, texture, and overall character of existing outcrops. Wooden retaining walls are better suited to sandy soils, both practically and aesthetically. They are relatively easy to build because they do not need extensive footings, and wood suits the weathered patina of the shore—echoing the color of driftwood and weathered shingles. Two-by-sixes of redwood or pressure-treated pine are sturdy enough to stand up to seaside elements, and railroad ties are inexpensive, readily available, and virtually indestructible, though they do not weather quite as nicely as ordinary wood.

Fences buffer wind effectively, as long as they are sturdy and semipermeable. The forty-to-sixty ratio of open to solid surface that is best for planted windbreaks also applies to fences; it is easily achieved with one-inch lattice strips, two-by-fours, or any number of different combinations. Redwood and cypress weather well with minimal maintenance. Pressure-treated pine is also a good candidate for seaside construction, particulary if sealed with a preservative like Cuprinol. Painted fences tend to blister in the sun and salt air and are best reserved for those willing to put in the extra effort of seasonal scraping, sanding, and repainting.

A simple post-and-rail fence surrounds Celia Thaxter's cutting garden, providing support for sweet peas, protection from foraging rabbits, and a perimeter for the orderly beds.

CHAPTER THREE

ELEMENTS OF DESIGN

OUTDOOR ROOMS AND AMENITIES

Although the seaside landscape is appealing, it is not always a pleasant place for people. Incessant wind, crashing waves, bright sun, and the endless ocean can be overwhelming without the relief of a comfortably cool place from which to enjoy them. People need shelter, just as plants do: They need outdoor spaces with walls to block the wind, and leafy canopies to ward off the midday sun, where sitting, dining, reading, and other outdoor pleasures can be pursued in comfort.

People, like plants, are most comfortable out of the wind. As onshore winds are characteristic of seaside places, the lee is likely to be on the inland side of a house or a stand of trees—away from the water and the view. That part of a waterfront site is typically the best place for entry and service functions as well. So, where winds are strong, the space on the lee side often serves as a place to park, a front door, *and* a comfortable outdoor room. Rooms and corridors can be troublesome to combine, however; where they overlap, the path should be clearly set apart from the place by a low wall, a hedge, a distinctive paving, or a row of flower-filled tubs.

For sunshine and warmth, the best exposures are eastern and western: They take advantage of the soft light of early morning and late afternoon without suffering through the intense heat of the midday sun. Since southern exposure can be uncomfortably hot and bright with the sparkling surface of water nearby, decks and terraces that face south will be far more livable if shaded by awnings or vine-covered trellises. The compass plays only a minor role in the orientation of seaside gardens, however. The most inviting spot will undoubtedly be the one that faces the water, and it is likely to feature maximum exposure with minimal comfort. Fortunately, the choice of structures that provide shelter is rich, and their addition greatly enhances the character as well as the comfort of seaside gardens.

Green walls, a floor highlighted with rose beds, and a distant view make a successful outdoor room at the Huntington Botanical Gardens.

Porches

Porches provide a place for enjoying views and summer breezes without giving up the comfort and protection of a roof. They go hand in hand with buildings, and as the architecture in seaside places ranges from the exotic to the ordinary, so do the accompanying porches. Fishermen's shacks have unpretentious porches with straight-backed deacon's benches; extravagant summer cottages are cloaked in wraparound verandas furnished with wicker, wide wooden swings, and baskets full of fuchsias hanging from robin's-egg blue ceilings. Wherever the porch, and whatever its style and appointments, the pleasures are essentially the same—shade, soothing breezes, and views.

Pool, loggia, and trees direct the view to the sea. Mark Berry, landscape architect.

Pergolas

Pergolas providing soft green shade can be useful either in association with a house or set alone in the landscape to direct attention to a special spot or spectacular view. They are particularly good features for the seaside, where the protective canopies of shade-giving trees are often sparse. Pergolas planted with wisteria, honeysuckle, roses, or wild clematis create particularly pleasant places, for their shade is not only cool but fragrant as well—and fragrance tends to linger in moist sea air. A combination of climbers ensures a long season of bloom and creates a spectacular display.

Terraces and Decks

Terraces and decks are outdoor rooms that carry the characteristics of buildings into the unbuilt landscape. Materials, lines, and styles should relate to both the architecture and the natural environment if the relationship is to be smooth. Certain environmental associations persist, however: Wooden decks work well on sandy shores, for instance, because they are easy to construct; stone terraces are better suited to rocky coastlines. Whatever the material, a low wall (sometimes called a seat wall) is a handsome edge and an invaluable addition to a terrace—particularly on the unseasonably warm days that are so typical by the shore, when lugging out portable chairs seems more trouble than it is worth. Eighteen inches is standard height for sitting, but the surface can be higher or lower depending on the grades in the garden and the preferences of the gardener.

A raised masonry plinth creates a room on the beach for a house in southern California. Mark Berry, landscape architect.

A stand of Ravenala madagascariensis *and a pergola create shade in Thomas Edison's garden on the gulf coast of Florida.*

Summerhouses

Summerhouses and gazebos belong further out in the garden where their role is two-fold: They provide a sequestered retreat, and they serve as a focal point that dresses up the garden landscape. Visually, they are the legacy of the landscape painters who used classical ruins, pavilions, and country churches to structure and enrich their compositions. But exotic buildings are part of the seaside tradition as well: From winter gardens in Southampton to bandshells at Coney Island, architectural follies have been created to spice up the experience of a holiday on the shore. What goes on inside the buildings has undoubtedly changed since the first spa opened on the English coast. Garden pavilions today are more likely to contain hot tubs than hothouses, but their striking silhouettes are still part of many garden landscapes.

A peaked-roofed gazebo stands alone on a promontory in a coastal garden, enhancing the water view while providing an inviting destination for those tempted to explore the cliffwalk.

Grounds for Games

Active recreation is another time-honored part of the seaside tradition, and developing the associated facilities is one of the most challenging aspects of developing a seaside space. If the character of the coastal environment is to be conserved, pools, courts, and cutting gardens will need to be skillfully woven into the garden fabric, so as not to compete with views. Lowering grades is an effective solution, both aesthetically and practically, for it reduces visibility and creates valuable enclosure without looking unnaturally structured. If lowering the level of the ground is too much of a task, a similar effect can be achieved with a slight rise in the surrounding grade. An earth mound or berm, a low wall, or a dense line of plants will shunt wind and wandering eyes.

Two spectacular trees, a giant sequoia and a purple beech, are ample ornament for a lawn on Narragansett Bay at Blithewold Gardens and Arboretum in Bristol, Rhode Island.

Swimming Pools

Pools deserve careful consideration by the shore, for contained water can look rigid and strikingly artificial juxtaposed against the open ocean. Scale is also problematic, as even the most generously proportioned pool is likely to look meager alongside the sea. One of the best solutions is to set the pool outside of the water view. Visual separation is practical as well, because it makes the associated fencing seem less intrusive. Pool fencing is a necessary safety feature—required by law in many places—and, along an exposed shoreline, a desirable amenity as well. Low walls and evergreen hedges create a comfortingly private pool perimeter, and they reduce wind at the water's edge.

If setting the pool in an isolated spot is impossible or inappropriate, the alternative is to relate the pool to the beach and ocean beyond. This calls for a far bolder scheme; in fact, the more brazen the connection, the better.

Lighting

Finally, outdoor spaces or "rooms"—such as porches, pergolas, and even rooms created by using plant materials as structural elements—need light. The glow from windows creates a flattering light for adjacent terraces and decks; but paths, stairs, and passageways may need to be highlighted for safe passage. A well-lit tree, a nearby pergola, or a piece of sculpture can be appealing sources of indirect light. Further into the landscape, spotlights can emphasize individual garden features. Specimen trees are the most natural subjects; pools, sculpture, and garden structures are also potential targets.

Lighting should be subtle, especially in front of a view, for anything brilliantly lit will obliterate darker, more distant landscape features. To achieve a soft effect with trees, landscape architect Philip Winslow advises that lights be put up and aimed down. He likes to set them above the first branch of existing trees so that the branch's shadow is cast on the ground below. The higher the light, the better, for it will create a more intricate tracery of shadows. Accompanying wires should be run up the back of the trunk where they will be least obtrusive.

Outdoor fixtures need not be expensive, according to Winslow, but wiring and outlets should be professionally installed. For maximum flexibility, he recommends that different types of outdoor lights be controlled by separate switches: Tree lights, low landscape lights, and security lights may all be useful, but they need not always be on at the same time. And, finally, Winslow emphasizes the importance of installing the control switch in a place that overlooks the lights, so that you can easily see whether they are on and in full working order.

Before embarking on an elaborate lighting program, however, remember that soft light is most becoming by the sea. It shimmers on the surface of the water and gleams in the misty air. Moonlight is the best model for waterside places, and perhaps the best source of light as well. Relying on the moon will leave the garden dark at times, but bright evenings will have a special, sparkling quality as a result.

A block-and-a-half from the water in Corpus Christi, sunken terraces create a series of outdoor rooms protected from the gusty winds that blow from the Gulf. The pool sits at the lowest level. Lights make the garden useful on mild Texas evenings. Ford, Powell & Carson, landscape architects.

THE PLANT PALETTE

A stand of Australian pines, Casuarina equisetifolia, *makes an invaluable windbreak, at Wreck Hill, Robert Stigwood's Bermuda garden.*

Trees

Trees provide shade, shelter, and privacy—the amenities that are at a premium by the shore. They also give a garden structure: Like the timbers that frame a house, they outline the plan. Trees present an interesting challenge, however, for in extremely exposed situations where they are often considered the most necessary, they are most difficult to establish. (Lack of trees, after all, is one of the char-acteristic features of a beach.) Once es-tablished, trees present a further dilemma: As they grow, they threaten to block views and constrict the expansive sense of space that gives the shore its unique appeal. Moderation is clearly the key with trees in seaside situations.

Suitability is essential, for trees are often part of the first line of defense, where they are exposed to the very toughest seaside condition. Salt-resistance, drought toler-ance, and ability to withstand gale-force winds are critical qualities for shelterbelt trees; for these reasons, native species are by far the most reliable for oceanfront planting. The more fragile exotics belong well within the garden, where they are protected. Specimen trees also belong in the center of the garden, where flowers and form can develop undisturbed and be admired in isolation.

Evergreens are particularly valuable seaside trees, for they are effective in win-ter when the landscape can be desolate and the wind extremely destructive. But whether evergreen or deciduous, trees are dominants in the open coastal land-scape—so much so that one mature maple or a massive beech can be enough to establish the sense of shelter and cultivation that we associate with gardens. Such simple planting is particularly striking as a foreground for an extraordinary water view.

Shrubs

Shrubs are well-suited for seaside planting, as most have a multibranched structure that is resistant to wind damage. And, being low growers, they are not likely to loom up in front of scenic views. Many of the shrubby species that are na-

Japanese black pine, Pinus thunbergii, *is a prized seaside plant; but susceptibility to disease threatens to ruin its reputation.*

The trumpetvines are a family of vigorous, wind-tolerant plants. This showy bloomer is Campsis grandiflora, *a warm weather species.*

tive to the shore also thrive in cultivated conditions—ceanothus, salt spray rose, and sea grape, for instance. These species are effective in transitional plantings, where the garden is woven into the fabric of the existing environment.

Shrubs provide excellent shelter, for their leaves and branches are low, providing protection where people and fledgling plants need it most. They have the advantage of being relatively easy to transplant and quick to grow. Shrubs are worthy of consideration not only as alternatives to trees, but also as supplements to herbaceous plantings because they tend to be quite tolerant of wind and drought. They are particularly useful in hedgerows, for they skirt the trunks of taller trees, reducing the scale and creating a protected harbor for the grasses, ferns, and flowers in their midst.

Roses

Roses are the classic seaside flowers, draping cottages and fences of weathered wood from Nantucket to New Zealand in their sweetly scented haze. We think of them as flowers, but in fact they are shrubs, for they are woody and capable of climbing, rambling, and creating substantial bushes. Roses are star performers by the sea, wallowing in the temperate climate and the cool, moist air. Salt may also be beneficial, according to rosarians who speculate that breezes laden with ocean spray discourage the many diseases that are prone to attack roses.

The most stalwart seaside rose is *Rosa rugosa*—the salt spray rose with exquisitely fragrant blooms, lustrous leaves, and tomato-colored hips. *R. rugosa* flourishes just above the high-water line, creating a thorny, sweet-scented thicket where few other plants survive. The species plant blossoms with a single flower of deep pink tending toward purple. A number of hybrids are available, sporting pale pink, white, or striated blooms, either single or double.

Many other roses thrive by the sea. The hardiest are the old-fashioned species roses, and although many of them bloom only once a year, they are reliable and suit the carefree look of many seaside gardens. *Rosa multiflora*, commonly known as the Japanese rose, is an arching shrub with masses of small red hips that has become invasive along some shores; *R. wichuriana* (memorial rose) is a low-growing, late-blooming species suitable for blanketing seaside slopes. The hybrid perpetuals are modern roses, bred for long blooming seasons and big, bold flowers. Floribundas are low growers, ideal for bedding or cloaking rough banks in veils of pastel blooms; grandifloras and polyanthas are also good bedding plants.

Undeniably, the most familiar seaside roses are the ones that carry their blossoms high above the windows of weathered cottages. This group includes both climbers and ramblers: The climbers produce large flowers, and the ramblers bear clusters of smaller blooms. Some of the roses have naturalized in seaside communities—the fairy, most notably, with its clusters of ruffled pale pink blooms—where they romp and ramble over stone walls, through privet hedges, and across thickets of native shrubs. Red cedars (*Juniperus virginiana*) provide a particularly striking support for climbing roses; contrary to many gardeners' fears, the intermingling does little harm to either plant.

Herbaceous Plants

The essence of herbaceous plants is flowers, and flowers are an intrinsic part of the allure of seaside gardens. They are the stars of many coastal plots, blooming both profusely and brilliantly and setting the garden apart from the native landscape far more effectively than any other single feature. More fundamentally, a flower's fragile beauty is exaggerated in the vast and inhospitable context of seaside surroundings. Fragile is an accurate perception, incidentally, as most of the plants that bloom in seaside borders are exotics. But a surprising number of herbaceous perennials take well to coastal climates—so well, in fact, that to see them in a successful seaside garden is to be convinced that, surely, plants do grow and flower most luxuriantly in the sun and salt air.

Flowers are most effectively displayed in beds, where the width is determined by the gardener's reach and the length by the time and energy available for planting, weeding, and the other tasks associated with keeping the ground neat and the blooms bountiful. If there is a view of water, the beds can run parallel to the shore, marking the end of a lawn or the line between the garden and the native landscape. Alternatively, beds can be set per-

For the Paley garden on Long Island, landscape designer Russell Page shaped a three-tiered bowl around an elliptical pool, and then planted the protected slopes with masses of spring-blooming azaleas beneath a canopy of dogwoods. Paths divide the tiers.

pendicular to the shore, creating a flowery axis that leads both feet and eyes to the water. Both schemes benefit from the addition of tall, spiky plants, which introduce a striking counterpoint to the line of the shore and the distant horizon.

Seaside conditions do not always allow for broad borders and emerald lawns, however, and seaside gardeners are not always willing to devote endless hours to manicuring beds. Big pots can provide enough nourishing soil to host a splash of summer color. The bright sun and constant breezes tend to dry them out quickly, however, so their plants should be tough enough to survive occasional dry spells. Wind-resistance is particularly important for container plants. For gardeners who don't want to be bothered with weekly watering, goldenrod, beach pea, chicory, Queen Anne's lace, black-eyed Susans, and dusty-miller can be encouraged to self-seed in open meadows—for they are dauntless wildings, determined to thrive in the most adverse conditions, with little or no attention.

Vines

Vines and climbing plants serve a variety of purposes. First, and perhaps foremost, they are—when given proper support—upright growers, and thus provide a vertical note that is often lacking by the shore. The most classic vines are perennials—wisteria, with its fragrant clusters of lavender flowers, grapes, climbing roses, clematis, and honeysuckles—that wrap themselves around pergolas and trellises, cloaking pillars and beams with veils of green. Morning glories, scarlet runner beans, moonflowers, and a host of other annual vines can be coaxed to grow quickly, creating green screens that provide shade and privacy—two amenities that are likely to be at a premium by the shore. Annual species also can help furnish a pergola while slower-growing perennials are getting established.

Flowering vines can be spectacular in trees—a practice that the English are far more comfortable with than Americans. Roses grown in red cedars was one of Gertrude Jekyll's signature combinations, set most often at the edge of a garden where the cultivated landscape merged with the surrounding woods. Red cedars thrive along the shore, and seaside gardeners need only look in untended meadows to see that the trees flourish beneath veils of native vines. Many of the vines that thrive by the shore can be incorporated into cultivated landscapes, although supervision is advisable because vines can be invasive once established. Wild grape, morning glory, everlasting pea, porcelain berry, and autumn-flowering clematis are but a few of the invasive vines that can be successfully contained and counted on to flourish in coastal conditions.

Herbs flourish at Findhorn, a Scottish community known for its extraordinary and unusual seaside gardens.

The landscape surrounding Exbury gardens in southern England, where expanses of grass and closely cropped fields exaggerate the flat terrain.

Ground Covers

Ground covers are gloss in many gardens, used as a finishing touch to give a polished sense of completion. But by the shore they are practical rather than merely decorative. They are almost an essential addition to a seaside garden, in fact, for they reduce moisture loss, keep the ground cool, and help anchor the soil by minimizing the scouring action of the wind.

Ground cover is a label that applies to function rather than form, as the plants it includes range from sturdy shrubs to rambling vines, grasses, and herbaceous plants. Poor soil and incessant wind can reduce medium-sized shrubs like beach plum and bayberry to dwarf proportions, rendering them effective ground covers in the most exposed situations. Low-growing junipers are among the most successful seaside ground covers—most notably, the varieties of *Juniperus conferta* or shore juniper. Junipers tolerate drought and salt spray, and their rough blue-green needles complement the muted grays and greens of many native seaside plants.

The most important ground cover for land along the shore is undoubtedly beach grass (*Ammophila* spp.), the tough, yellow-green grass that colonizes dunes from Alaska to Australia. Beach grass is an invaluable anchor, for it has a fibrous root system that traps sand in place. Once established, it plays a substantial role in reducing dune erosion and creating footing for other pioneer seaside plants. Establishing beach grass is one of the first steps in making a garden in the dunes—and in many oceanside communities, it is actually required by law, in an effort to control erosion. Beach grass is being grown by an increasing number of nurseries. Sources and methods for establishing it successfully are available either from local growers or from the Soil Conservation Service. The SCS is generally listed in telephone directories under "United States Government, Department of Agriculture."

Lawns

Moisture is essential to the creation of a successful lawn, and a moderate climate is a great boon. Fortunately for gardeners and their grass, those conditions prevail by the sea. Salt is destructive, however: Whether in the form of spray or sea water, it burns grass and spoils the effect of a clean sweep of lawn. Periodic leaching with fresh water can be beneficial, particularly after storms; a reliable sprinkler system is helpful in the most parched or exposed situations. The selection of a hardy, salt-tolerant grass is the most fundamental step toward a successful seaside lawn, however. Here, as in every aspect of seaside gardening, even the most vigilant maintenance cannot compensate for a poor match between plant and locale.

Above: St. Augustine is a coarsely textured vivid green grass favored for southern lawns. It tolerates sun, shade, and salty air, but is susceptible to a number of pests and diseases. **Below:** *Dichondra is a weed when discovered in grass, but grown by itself it proves to be a satisfactory lawn—somewhat easier to care for than the more conventional southern grasses.*

Above: Zoysia is a tough, prickly grass, not as handsome as St. Augustine, but far more resistant to disease and drought. It tends to form hummocky clumps if not mowed regularly. **Below:** *American beach grass, Ammophila breviligulata, is important to many coastal communities—the fibrous roots anchor sand, and slender leaves force breezes to drop tiny windblown particles.*

COLOR

Color gives flowers their sparkle, and that sparkle is particularly impressive by the sea. Pinks seem pinker, blues bluer, and whites more effervescent in the misty air. Many venerable flower gardeners have insisted that color is more brilliant by the sea than anywhere else, and their explanations range from rational to visionary. Most likely, the brilliance is related to the dazzling quality of seaside light. Light seems to shine from every direction near the shore, as it is reflected from rippling water, wave-washed rocks, and gleaming white sand. Every flicker of the sun is mirrored in the sea, and given the movement of clouds and cold fronts, such changes are constant. Finally, the moist air tempers seaside light, transforming the harsh glare to a constant haze—or thick fog, in extreme conditions—that also changes the perception of garden colors.

Perhaps color is exaggerated against the background of blue-green sea and bright sand; certainly, the lush tones of cultivated plants gleam against the yellowish and glossy greens of scrub vegetation. A few seaside gardeners have suggested that plants are somehow different by the shore—that they are exceptionally vigorous and that their vigor results in vivid blooms. Celia Thaxter humbly credited the rock in the soil of her coastal island for the brilliance of her flower beds.

Whatever the source of dazzling seaside color, the theories about using it to best advantage are as diverse as the explanations of its origins. Some gardeners surrounded by yellowish sand or rock avoid yellow and orange flowers; others argue that plants look lovely against stone of any kind, in any of its stages (including sand). The truth is that stones, rocks, and sands vary. Some are lovely and weathered, with soft grays, pearly pinks, or perhaps the greens of lichen, while others are jarringly brassy.

Native plants can inspire seaside palettes, and they tend to bloom in whites

Whale bones and the ribs of a battered boat are sculptural additions to the beach in Myron Hokin's garden on Virgin Gorda. Color is provided by the everchanging play of water and sky.

and pale pinks. Whites are not entirely satisfactory at the water's edge, however, for they do not stand up to sharp reflections and shimmering light, and they disappear almost entirely in fog. Gardeners who have to contend with frequent fog find that pinks and bright colors are far more effective beacons. Vivid hues are favored in many fog-free gardens as well, for they stand out against the crystalline brilliance of clear seas and cloudless skies.

Pastels also lend themselves well to seaside gardens, for they complement the mistiness characteristic of the coast. More important, they suit the seaside environment. Pale yellows, muted pinks, and periwinkle blues blend with the waterfront palette, for they have the soft look that comes with weathering. Subtle colors have the additional benefit of reflecting changes in light, and that makes them especially appropriate for seaside plantings.

Above left: *A flaming red azalea draws attention beyond an arched bridge to a long view at Exbury Gardens. The colorful flowers offset the gleaming white, effectively preventing the bridge from dominating the landscape scene.* **Left:** *Boxwood and a picket fence surrounding a pool create a striking frame for a multicolored border. Alice Ireys, landscape architect.* **Above:** *Bluebells and banks of white rhododendrons modulate Exbury's rich reds and pinks.*

Blues, which are prized in any garden, are especially treasured by the shore, for they echo the sea and sky and thereby weave the garden into the surrounding scenery. Alice Martineau frequented seaside villas and gardens in the 1920s and shared her experience in *The Secrets of Many Gardens*. She captured the effect of blue in her description of a garden with pansies, Japanese irises, delphiniums, nepeta, and *Salvia patens*. "Beyond this little formal garden was a vista of blue sea and grey rocks," she explains. "On some low rocks in the foreground, large blue cushions reproduced the note of the sea and sky behind, while a cloud of blue air balls—rising, falling—all in the same blue, made one catch one's breath with the amazing beauty of such a riot of color and sunshine."

Color in gardens is not confined to flowers, however. Foliage is specially important, for it adds interesting tones and textures and carries borders through periods of limited bloom. Glaucous blue-greens and silvery leaves the color of driftwood complement the tones of a muted seaside palette. Gray leaves are worth incorporating into any color scheme, for they are well-adapted to the shore. Their gray look is the result of tiny hairs that protect the leaf from salt damage and moisture loss.

CHAPTER FOUR

PRACTICAL PRINCIPLES

PLANNING PRELIMINARIES

In principle, planning a seaside garden is not much different than planning a garden futher inland: In the best cases, the design develops in response to the existing conditions. Seaside ecosystems are fragile, however, and upsetting natural balances can have disastrous results in terms of erosion, flooding, and hurricane damage. So before embarking on elaborate plans, gardeners with land that abuts the ocean, a beach, or a tidal estuary should be aware of potential problems and familiarize themselves with any restrictive covenants or legislation that may pertain to their property. A logical first step is to establish exactly where waterfront property begins. Some deeds run to the mean high-water mark, others include the ground above mean low tide. Whichever ruling applies, chances are that joggers and beachcombers have rights to the land below the high-tide line, and any waterfront plan should take them into consideration.

Landscape work that involves altering dunes or removing native vegetation is likely to be subject to restrictions set up by the Coastal Zone Management Act—a federally mandated program that puts management of seaside land in the hands of local governments. Not every seaboard state has a Coastal Zone Program, but those that do usually list it, along with state government offices, under the Natural Resources Department or the Department of Environmental Protection. The Army Corps of Engineers has jurisdiction over coastal land where erosion, flooding, or hurricanes present potential hazards. The Soil Conservation Service has also been involved in efforts to minimize erosion and manages several programs devoted to identifying and improving salt-tolerant plants. The SCS and your local native plant society will be able to assist you in making suitable plant choices for the garden.

Some communities have enacted spe-

An impeccably planned garden, with a year-round framework established in rock and evergreens. Interesting leaves take the place of color once flowers fade. Hideo Sasaki, landscape architect.

cial zoning codes or have designed guidelines to protect beachfront property from overdevelopment and ecological abuse. Vulnerability to storm and hurricane damage, erosion, and runoff are typical points of concern; setting standards for visual quality is a less common goal, but it is considered a legitimate zoning consideration in an increasing number of cases. If any rules or regulations do pertain to your property, a few exploratory telephone calls made in the early planning stages can ensure that work runs smoothly once started.

Constructing the Garden

In light, sandy soil, anchoring plants can be a significant challenge. That challenge is exaggerated along the beach, where shifting sands make the job doubly difficult. The situation is not altogether different along rocky shores where a limited supply of organic material makes planting extremely hard and reduces the soil's ability to retain moisture. In both sand and rock, building up stable pockets of fertile soil can be a major undertaking. Such projects often involve construction, and if the final product is to "fit," the new features and materials should suit the site's natural character. That match is not easy to make, for the most permanent solutions usually require masonry construction, and masonry is not only difficult to anchor in sand but also can be awkward to work into the soft and shifting topography of the beach. Along rocky shores, new construction looks most comfortable if built in native stone. If indigenous rock is not available, the material should be carefully selected either to match or contrast with the surrounding outcrops.

Wood is an appropriate material to use by the shore: It is easy to work with, inexpensive to replace, and aesthetically pleasing, for it weathers quickly, taking on silvery gray tones that suit the sea. Redwood, pressure-treated pine, and cypress are the toughest woods for the construction of decks, boardwalks, and seaside planters. Railroad ties are suitable for steps and retaining walls, and they are virtually impervious to the elements.

For paths and driveways, sand-colored pebbles or crushed native stone are logical choices. Crushed shells are harder to find, but they do make a lovely, understated surface. Asphalt and concrete seem too urban for the shore, as do unit paving stones like cobbles or brick. Unless they match the style and construction of the adjacent house, unit pavers are best left for more formal settings.

Soil Preparation

Like plants everywhere, seaside plants need solid, fertile footing. If the ground is sandy or rocky, it will need improvement before it becomes a hospitable place for ornamental plants to grow. Good garden soil must contain moisture and nutrients, and for that, a healthy supply of organic matter is essential. Unfortunately, organic matter is precisely what seaside soils tend to lack. Periodic addition of peat moss, manure, grass clippings, and leaf mold will enhance tilth and texture. An ongoing compost pile is an invaluable resource, converting garden and kitchen debris into a rich organic dressing that is ideal for seaside soils.

In extreme situations, or for plants that demand the very best possible soil, an intensive method of cultivating can be effective. Alice Martineau visited a seaside rose garden in Newport, Rhode Island with precisely dug beds that she could

A Massachusetts garden grown in a raised bed provides good footing for a selection of heaths and heathers. Sedums, dwarf evergreens, artemesias, and a few fieldstones vary the plant palette.

only compare to graves: Each was excavated to a depth of about four feet, then spread with a thick layer of leaves or other "green rubbish" that served as a makeshift plug to prevent rapid filtration of water. Cow manure, bone meal, and good loamy soil were added on top of the leaves. The results were apparently spectacular. "In fact," Mrs. Martineau confessed, "so well grown were these roses ...that I positively failed to recognize many old favorites...." (*The Secrets of Many Gardens*). She recommended the "grave" method for any sandy or gravelly soil.

Selecting Seaside Plants

A simple garden of flowers—some annual, some perennial, and some wild—suits the Maine coast.

Hydrangea macrophylla *is a seaside classic.*

Plans for seaside gardens can vary almost endlessly, but the plants cannot. In order to survive by the shore, they must be able to tolerate drought, heat, and occasional saltwater saturations. Given the extreme environment they grow in, many seaside plants share a number of similarities. This phenomenon is called parallel evolution: In response to similar conditions, plants take on similar characteristics—and those similarities are an invaluable guide to anyone selecting material for a garden on the ocean.

Many seaside plants have small leaves, because small leaves allow the wind to sift through easily, without much tearing or battering. A reduced leaf surface is an efficient adaptation to seaside conditions, for it minimizes water loss and vulnerability to damage by salt spray. Evergreen needles are also specially adapted to minimize moisture loss. They do well in wind, too, for even the most blustery gale is likely to filter through the fine foliage, causing little damage.

Several other leaf adaptations reduce plants' vulnerability to salt damage. Tough, glossy foliage has a cuticle, or protective layer, that is resistant to salt. Given a choice of fruit trees, for instance, seaside gardeners would do best to stick with glossy-leaved pears and a few stalwart varieties of apple rather than try to nurture cherries, almonds, and apricots. Fuzziness on a leaf is also a protective device, for tiny hairs trap salt particles and keep them from reaching the tender surface of the foliage. *Elaeagnus, Artemisia, Stachys,* and *Caryopteris* are just a few of the genera that include gray-leaved plants tolerant of seaside conditions.

Scaliness is another protective mechanism that limits moisture loss and reduces exposure to salt. The *Casuarina equistefolia,* or Australian pine, which has colonized the coastal areas of southern Florida, is a prime example, for although it actually is not a pine, it has adopted piney characteristics in order to survive in dry conditions. Heaths and heathers are two more examples of scaly leaved plants that are tolerant of heat and drought.

Succulence is a feature that helps plants survive extended periods of drought, and although it is one that we tend to associate with deserts and cacti, it is characteristic of several seashore plants. Glasswort (*Salicornia* spp.) lives in marshes, subject to daily saltwater baths that would overpower most plants; portulaca and sedums store enough moisture in their plump leaves to enable them to survive parching in sandy soil.

All seaside plants tend to have extensive root systems that delve deep into the soil, searching for moisture, and many have single taproots that provide a direct pipeline to the cool depths where groundwater is increasingly plentiful. Long taproots compound the difficulties of transplanting; for that reason, small plants are the best candidates for moving in dry conditions. Roots with rhizomes or stolons are advantageous on sandy shores, incidentally, for they effectively anchor loose particles of sand and soil.

Branching patterns also seem characteristic by the sea, as many plants are dwarfed by the incessant winds, limited water, and poor soil. Presumably, this habit is a reaction to the seaside environment rather than adaptation, but it is characteristic nonetheless. Although trees and shrubs by the sea tend to be dwarfed as a result of the inhospitable conditions, they have the benefit of being more densely branched and are often far more floriferous than their sheltered counterparts.

In the search for plants that are adapt-able to the seaside environment, one other feature is worth considering—the plant's scientific name. *Maritima* and *marinus* are species names that incorporate the Latin word for sea, and any plant so named is likely to thrive along the coast. Other names describe conditions that are likely to apply to seaside situations. *Atlantica* means of the Atlantic region, *pacifica* relates to the Pacific; *corsica*

A combination of day lilies, sweet peas, poppies, coreopsis, and foxgloves in the island garden that Celia Thaxter tended, painted, and wrote about.

and *cretica* tie their subjects to the Mediterranean. Any species labeled *arenarius* is found growing in sand; *palustris* means of marshes and wetlands; and the prefix *hali* has to do with salt. Perusing Latin names is not an efficient way to go about choosing plants, by any means, but being familiar with scientific nomenclature helps identify things like *Rosmarinus*, *Eryngium maritimum*, and *Cedrus atlantica* cv. 'Glauca' as suitable seaside subjects.

Planting Methods

Start small and think big is the best approach to seaside planting. Plants should not be too large when they are set out, for the hardiest seaside specimens are those that have been adapting to harsh conditions since the seedling stage, gradually acquiring appropriate habits such as

dense, woody branches and extensive roots. In terms of planting, many gardeners have found that density is the key to a successful seaside plot. Seaside gardeners everywhere would do well to follow the example of Celia Thaxter, a dauntless nineteenth-century woman who tended her garden on an exposed island off the coast of Maine. Despite the diminutive size of her plot, Miss Thaxter always planted in sets of two, hoping that at least

A selection of annuals fills a woven basket, welcoming visitors with a bouquet of silvery dusty-miller, impatiens, begonias, and starry purple lobelia.

Spires of yellow snapdragons and a vivid assortment of red and white petunias fill wooden tubs in a Block Island garden, burgeoning in the shelter and reflected warmth of an adjacent wall.

planting is an even better solution, for the plants will be well-established by the time late winter storms batter coastal gardens. Deciduous trees are more adaptable and can be planted in early spring or late fall. Moisture is the critical factor in transplanting them, and as long as it is in plentiful supply, the risk of loss is significantly reduced. Water the entire plant, not just the roots, to offset the loss of moisture through leaves and woody tissue. Wrapping trunks with burlap or heavy paper also reduces the rate of transpiration. Pruning back the branches of deciduous trees and shrubs futher limits the surface from which moisture can be lost, and it encourages strong branches and roots that serve seaside plants well in wind and winter storms.

Herbaceous plants are less finicky when it comes to being moved. They can be shifted around almost anytime if they are given adequate moisture and some protection from the sun on hot days. Finally, before preparing any plants for transplanting, check to see if a deep taproot is typical of the species. If so, your task will be doubly difficult because the main root tends to run quite deep. Be certain to retain as much of the root as possible by digging deep; once the plant is in its new place, water it regularly.

A container garden in the Cape Cod dunes.

one of each pair would survive "the hard fates" that threatened her flowers. A dense mass of plants stands up to gusty winds, for its many stems not only buffer wind but act as natural stakes as well, making it virtually impossible for any single one to bend. With this principle in mind, flower fanciers would do well to incorporate some stiff woody plants in their herbaceous borders, as their branches cradle the stems of more fragile plants.

Opinions vary as to the best time of year for transplanting by the shore. Evergreens are traditionally planted in the fall, and though they are likely to survive frosts, they often succumb to the cold, salty blasts that accompany spring storms. Applying a wilt-proofing spray in the fall is a useful antidote, according to nurseryman Michael Graham; but he feels that late spring

ONGOING CARE

Feeding

Delphinium grow in a sheltered spot alongside irises, daisies, and campanula.

Although seaside soils often lack nutrients, massive doses of fertilizer are not a particularly effective antidote. Frequent applications of small doses is the best method for feeding seaside plants, as it ensures that food will get to the plants rather than leaching quickly through the soil. Overfeeding makes seaside plants vulnerable rather than strong: It encourages weak, leggy growth that is easily damaged in storms or drought. Thus in growing, as in planning a garden by the sea, nature proves to be the best model. The plants best adapted to seaside conditions manage with minimal nutrients. Stunted, gnarled growth is the result, and it serves plants well in the face of wind and hot sun.

Sedum and grasses in a Long Island garden. Oehme & van Sweden, landscape architects.

Watering

Climbing roses cloak a Nantucket cottage in a haze of fragrant blossoms.

Fresh water can be a rare commodity by the sea and, consequently, proper watering is critical. Deep soakings are best for seaside plants, for they ensure adequate moisture and encourage roots to delve deep for water. The alternative—frequent sprinklings—is a recipe for disaster in dry conditions; it draws roots to the surface where they will be baked in a period of extended drought or extreme heat.

Deep watering also helps leach the salts that are likely to accumulate in seaside soils. Salts are left behind as water percolates through the porous grains of sandy soils; as these can be toxic to plants, periodic freshwater leachings are essential. A thorough soaking with fresh water is also a good treatment in the wake of flooding, for it rids the soil of accumulated salts.

Mulching

Mulches hold moisture in the ground, and they help anchor the soil, which in turn helps keep plants down—all great benefits in seaside gardens. Essentially, ground covers act as green mulches. The salt hay that washes ashore in winter storms is probably the most familiar seaside mulch. It is reasonably priced or, along many beaches, free for the asking; it is available in plentiful quantities every spring; and it has the extra advantage of carrying very few weed seeds. Cocoa hulls, chipped wood, shredded bark, pine needles and beach stones are also effective mulches. The heavier the mulching material, the more resistant it will be to wind, and thus the more useful in exposed situations and alongside pools.

Mulching is also one of the keys to a successful weekend garden, for it is a boon to people with limited time for weeding and watering. A plot protected by a thick layer of mulch should survive with just two weekly waterings—one Friday night and one Sunday evening—provided that they are deep and augmented by occasional rains. Mulch also prevents weeds from establishing a firm foothold—a quality that endears it to the legions of seaside gardeners who would rather be sailing than weeding.

hug the California coastline.

As for timing and technique, pruning is a place-specific project. The best source for specific information regarding a precise area is a local nurseryman, though a few general principles do tend to apply to seaside gardens. Many trees and shrubs are best pruned shortly after they have flowered because removing spent blossoms cleans the plant and keeps it from

channelling energy into the production of seed. This applies both to plants by the sea and to those inland, but given long, lingering falls tempered by the water's warmth, late-season pruning is best postponed until spring in seaside situations. New flushes of tender growth appear in the wake of pruning shears, and those that start late are most liable to be nipped by frost.

Pruning

Pruning is the prescription that protects seaside plants from excessive wind damage. The point of pruning is to keep things strong, so that they can break the wind rather than be broken by it. Once again, nature is the pruner's best model, and so a quick glance at the surrounding trees is a good place to start. A smooth contour on the exposed side is characteristic of a windswept silhouette because protruding branches are likely to be snapped by sudden gusts. In contrast, the branches on the lee side can look extremely contorted—a pattern best illustrated by the cragged Monterey pines that

Privet sheared into fanciful shapes at Green Animals in Portsmouth, Rhode Island.

Perennial phlox and shasta daisies in a midsummer garden perched high above the water. Alyssum and nepeta hug the ground, softening the line between the border and the pebble path.

A snow fence set up around an exposed evergreen shrub helps block drying winds and protects branches from being broken by the weight of drifting snow.

Prescriptions for Storms

Seaside storms bring gusty winds that carry salt and sand—a combination that can spell disaster for coastal gardens. Salt is the most destructive element, as it is carried quite far inland to places where the plants are less likely to be chosen for their ability to withstand salty spray. In the wake of a storm that has blown salt spray, the first task is to rinse plants thoroughly, according to John Holmes of American Tree Care. Corrective pruning should be done immediately, and a soil test taken to determine the best remedy for salt-saturated ground. To counteract the drying effect of windblown salt, American Tree Care recommends applying an antidessicant or wax (Wilt-pruf, Vaporguard, or Envy are effective) to both broad-leaved and needled evergreens. When storms come long before frost is due, an antidessicant applied to windswept deciduous trees helps keep buds from scorching. Many plants will survive an occasional battering, no matter how miserable they look just after the storm. Time is an effective cure: In all but the worst cases, it pays to wait a season and see just how quickly the plant generates new growth.

When it comes to storm damage, however, preventive action is the most effective strategy. Good maintenance is the best preparation for high winds: Weak limbs should be pruned and cabled, as necessary, and rotten crotches should be drained. Periodic thinning of deciduous canopies minimizes wind resistance and is recommended in any seaside situation. Naturally, avoiding weak-structured trees is by far the most effective antidote.

Roots are a tree's most important asset in high winds; if they have not developed properly, their effectiveness as anchors is compromised. In sandy seaside soils where the water table is typically high, Holmes finds that trees do not develop deep-root systems. Well-structured lateral roots are essential, as a result, and their growth is dependent upon proper handling at planting time. Roots should be trimmed and encouraged to grow away from the tree. Most important, the circling fibrous roots that are characteristic of pot-bound plants should be unraveled. If not, they develop into big roots that can eventually encircle and choke the tree. This effect is most apparent in the wake of storms, when toppled trees broken at this "girdle" line lie as evidence of improper planting.

Winter Protection

Many of the plants that tolerate seaside conditions are tough and perfectly capable of surviving winter without assistance. The exceptions are the exotic species of only marginal hardiness that can be coaxed to grow by the shore. Winter is the critical season for them, and protection is often a necessity. Thorough pruning is a step in the right direction, for when done properly, it keeps winter damage to a minimum. Wrapping is a more familiar method of protecting plants from wind, snow, and ice. A porous material like burlap is best, for it breathes, allowing a constant flow of fresh air around the plant. Plastic is an unsatisfactory wrap because it traps condensing moisture and prevents circulation, thereby encouraging the spread of disease.

Winter protection can be applied at ground level as well. A permanent mulch spread before winter strikes serves as a blanket, holding warmth in the soil. Freezing occurs more gradually, as a result, and the depth of frost is far less than in unmulched beds. A few fall soakings are also invaluable for plants about to weather a cold winter—and for new plants, a regular schedule of thorough late-season watering is virtually essential.

Loosely woven cloth is an ideal wrap for tender trees and shrubs because it breathes. Plastic, on the other hand, is not such a good material to use: Moisture condenses inside the plastic, and in the course of freezing and thawing is likely to damage buds and fragile tissues.

CHAPTER FIVE

OUTSTANDING EXAMPLES

OEHME, VAN SWEDEN & ASSOCIATES

This garden lies just inland from the ocean, on the edge of a brackish pond where water, sky, and dunes on the horizon are the dominant landscape elements. The challenge was to introduce a garden that would be interesting throughout the year and, at the same time, defer to the Long Island scenery. "We didn't want to take anything away from the drama of the site," explains landscape architect James van Sweden. That meant keeping the garden simple. This garden is an extraordinary interpretation of simplicity, however. It is expressed in unusual plants grouped in great sweeps scaled to suit the open landscape. The bold solution pleased the people involved every bit as well as it suited the site. The clients, Mr. and Mrs. Alex Rosenberg, are Manhattan art delaers and devoted gardeners; the designers, Oehme, van Sweden & Associates, are known for their dazzling combinations of dramatic plants.

The plan began with a pool set at the lowest level of the site—a place that is naturally protected and peripheral to the primary view. The pool surface was blackened, nonetheless, to minimize the contrast between the structure and the natural terrain. Peripheral locations are particularly advantageous for pools that are exposed in winter, van Sweden points out, for when empty they sit like scars in the barren landscape. The Rosenbergs' pool is surrounded by a flagstone terrace, amply proportioned to suit the scale of the seaside environment and to avoid the awkward sensation of being edged into the water that van Sweden feels is typical of too many poolside spaces. A few simple steps connect the pool area to an existing terrace, and the two spaces are wrapped in a broad border full of flowers, herbaceous plants, and ornamental grasses. A small lawn serves primarily as a foil between the border and the brackish water, and against the far side of the house, a tidy line of fenced beds protects herbs, vegetables, and flowers for cutting from hungry rabbits.

The herbaceous plants and grasses that fill the border are the hallmark of Oehme, van Sweden gardens, and their success in this seaside plan stems from some of their most basic properties. Herbaceous plants are seasonal: They provide protection around the pool in summertime, when privacy is most desirable, and their growth has an airy, transparent quality that suits the open seaside setting. Their scale is predictable, for each season brings a standard amount of growth, and thus the plants will never choke out the view or limit the sense of openness that is so characteristic of seaside places. Finally, grasses and herbaceous plants respond to the environment far more sensitively than other sorts of plants do: They change with the seasons, rustle in the wind, shimmer in the mist, and glisten in the low afternoon sun.

Masses of sedum and lavender line the steps between the pool and the terrace, punctuated by spires of creamy colored Spanish bayonet, a sweet bay tree, and clumps of molinia grass.

A willow, one of the garden's few trees, is placed at the edge of the view toward the water, where it shelters the section of the garden devoted to vegetable and cutting beds. A broad sweep of yarrow and a lawn serve as a simple foreground for the view.

The plants suit the place, and that reflects one of Oehme and van Sweden's fundamental principles. Each spot in a garden is right for only certain plants, according to Wolfgang Oehme, whose role as designer is to recognize the best possible combinations. "You must know where a plant belongs, aesthetically and horticulturally; it should look happy growing there," Mr. Oehme explains. That happiness manifests itself not only in a comfortable plan, but in easy maintenance as well—a situation in which the gardener can simply "let the plant go and be itself," he adds.

In the Rosenberg garden, the richest plantings are grouped around the pool, where people are most likely to linger and admire details at close range. Masses of yellow coneflowers (*Rudbeckia fulgida* var. *Sullivantii* 'Goldsturm'), English lavender (*Lavandula vera*), loosestrife (*Lythrum salicaria* 'Mordens Pink'), and fountain grass (*Pennisetum alopecuroides*) are punctuated by mounds of yucca and slender eulalia grass (*Miscanthus gracillimus*), with its great plumes waving above the flowers. The planting around the main terrace is far simpler, with a band of fountain grass that runs into a mass of *Sedum telephium* 'Autumn Joy' and creates a striking frame for the distant view.

Trees play a minor role in this garden. The perimeter of the property is lined with Japanese black pine, and a few small specimen trees have been introduced to add some variety to the herbaceous palette. The Rosenbergs didn't feel the need for shade, van Sweden recalls, and they were committed to preserving the expansive feeling of the seaside landscape—an openess that is attributable, in large part, to the lack of trees.

Lighting enhances the garden year-round, and it consists of a flexible combination of spotlights and low mushroom fixtures plugged into outlets arranged at fifteen-foot intervals throughout the beds.

The nighttime scenery is most dramatic in winter, when the grasses that have bleached to gold gleam in the snowbound landscape.

An irrigation system keeps plants healthy, and an annual application of three or four inches of mulch eventually breaks down into humus that enriches the soil. The mulch is not spread around the pool, although Oehme and van Sweden like to plant right up to one edge of the water, using plants that will spill over and soften the harsh line of the coping. An organic mulch would blow and wreak havoc with the pool's filtering system, so a good-sized gravel is the Oehme, van Sweden solution.

The surprises that came with gardening so close to the sea were few and pleasant, according to James van Sweden (whose firm, incidentally, is best known for work in city gardens). The plants that Oehme and van Sweden like to use manage beautifully in the wind, and they seem not to mind the salty air. In fact, Mr. van Sweden is astonished by how very well things have done—ligularia has burgeoned, the lavenders, sedums, and caryopteris have bloomed with abandon. He has learned that sandy soil can be a blessing—particularly for the gray-leaved plants that are so lovely in misty weather. And, like so many gardeners before him, he has come away convinced that plants grow more beautifully by the sea than anywhere else.

*Above: A canvas umbrella provides shade without restricting the openness that the owners and designers felt was essential to the seaside site. **Below:** Pennisetum and miscanthus spill over the bluestone coping.*

Selected Plant List

("Spp.," the plural abbreviation for species, indicates that several species within the genus are used.)

TREES

Amelanchier canadensis	shadblow
Magnolia virginiana	sweet bay magnolia
Oxydendrum arboreum	sourwood
Pyrus Calleryana 'Bradford'	Bradford pear
Styrax japonicus	Japanese snowbell

SHRUBS

Caryopteris x clandonensis	hybrid bluebeard
Cytisus x praecox 'Moonlight'	moonlight broom
Hamamelis mollis	Chinese witch hazel
Lavandula vera	English lavender
Perovskia atriplicifolia	Russian sage
Yucca filamentosa	Adam's needle

GRASSES

Festuca ovina var. 'glauca'	blue fescue
Miscanthus gracillimus	slender eulalia grass
Miscanthus sinensis var. gracillimus	maiden grass
Miscanthus sinensis	eulalia grass
Pennisetum alopecuroides	fountain grass
Spodiopogon sibiricus	ornamental grass

PERENNIALS

Achillea filipendulina 'Parker'	fernleaf yarrow
Cerastostigma plumbaginoides	blue plumbago
Hosta spp.	plantain lilies
Ligularia dentata cv. 'Desdemona'	golden bay
Lythrum Salicaria 'Mordens Pink'	loosestrife
Rudbeckia fulgida var. Sullivanti 'Goldsturm'	yellow coneflower
Sedum telephium 'Autumn Joy'	showy sedums

EDWARD PINCKNEY/ASSOCIATES LTD.

A raised bench, a place to rinse sandy feet, and a stepped boardwalk mark the transition from garden to beach. Hinged joints make the platforms adjustable to changes in sand or water.

of a general plan that would help restore the windblown dune.

The single expansive space was broken into several small areas, each with a specific function and character. Terraces ease the transition from the house to the lawn, providing places for cooking and eating outdoors. A circular pergola protects the hot tub, and its columns and low eaves afford privacy without closing in the view. The pool wraps around the curving line of an existing terrace wall, and a simple coping and dark surface ensure that the contained water lies low, visually, and doesn't compete with the brilliant blue of the Atlantic Ocean.

The series of small spaces establishes a comfortably human scale, and their uncomplicated handling creates a simple foreground for the view that is undoubtedly the site's most spectacular feature. The separate areas flow smoothly into one another, creating continuity, and they are treated consistently, with materials that were featured in the existing plan. Old Savannah brick, flagstone paving, and redwood benches provide structure in the more architectural section of the garden, and a restricted palette of native and naturalized plants ties the beds and perimeter plantings to the surrounding landscape.

Features are low, in keeping with the profile of the beach, and privacy and protection are minimal concerns as a result. Dense vegetation along the lot lines and new planting on the reestablished dune screen views into the property, eliminating the need for disruptive fencing. Sunshine and ocean breezes are welcome: Rather than opting for shade and extensive windbreaks that would detract from the open quality of the beach, the owners were content to depend on the pool for relief from the hot sun, according to project landscape architect Perry L. Wood.

Access to the water is by way of a stepped boardwalk—an ingenious detail that wraps path, terrace, and dune-

Hilton Head is an extraordinary stretch of barrier beach dotted with palms, oaks, oleander, privet, and beach grass. But, despite the spectacular setting, this was a very ordinary oceanfront yard when Edward Pinckney/Associates Ltd. was called in to redesign it. The garden was a three-sided box with a water view: The house and terrace defined the inland edge, dense stands of native vegetation crowded the property lines, and a low dune devastated by a recent hurricane marked the transition to the beach.

The landscape architects' task was to make the yard an inviting place—which to the owner meant adding a swimming pool, a hot tub, a terrace for sunbathing, and enough room for entertaining. Providing access to the beach was also part of the program, and the path was to be part

building windbreak into one clean-lined package. Boardwalks keep feet above the sand, protecting both dune and vegetation from erosion. This boardwalk plays an active role in replenishing the dune, as well, for sand is continuously being deposited on its windward side. The raised platform provides a striking view, and with the addition of a bench it becomes a pleasant place for sitting—particularly in the evening, as the wind dies down and dusk settles over the beach. The lower level on the water side includes a place for rinsing sandy feet. From there, the walkway snakes across the dune in a series of hinged platforms specially designed to weather the high waters that come in the wake of tropical storms.

Reconstruction of the dune began with the earth excavated from the swimming pool, and is continuously supplemented by windblown sand trapped by a dense line of dwarf yaupon holly (*Ilex vomitoria* 'Nana') and Parson's juniper (*Juniperus chinensis* cv. 'Parsonii')—plants chosen for their extreme tolerance for salt and proficiency in anchoring shifting sands. Eventually the holly and juniper will form a low

line of green, in keeping with the undulating silhouettes of the dunes beyond; until then, the beds are mulched with native pine straw that helps retain moisture and reduce the amount of windblown sand.

Work on the dune area was subject to the approval of a local architectural review board, because the land is part of a development that formed a special trust authority to protect the ground that lies between the private property lines and the mean high-water mark. In South Carolina, the zone subject to the state Coastal Council's jurisdiction lies between the mean high-water and low-water lines.

Despite the uncomplicated plan and planting, this is hardly a low-maintenance garden. Onshore winds bring a constant barrage of salty spray that takes its toll on even the hardiest plants, and they carry far more sand than the perimeter plants can capture. Sand constantly has to be removed from the lawn, planting beds, and boardwalk, and the pool is equipped with a special sweeping mechanism. Even that maintenance seems minimal, however, in light of the pleasure that comes with being at home and on the beach.

Above: A raised brick wall and a pergola enhances views to and from the spa. Center: Sabal palmettos frame the water view. Below: Existing trees provide shade and privacy for the terrace.

Selected Plant List

TREES	
Sabal palmito	sabal palmetto

SHRUBS	
Ilex vomitoria 'Nana'	dwarf yaupon holly
Juniperus chinensis cv. 'Parsonii'	Parson's juniper
Nerium Oleander 'Cardinal Red'	Cardinal Red oleander
Pittosporum tobira	Japanese pittosporum
Yucca aloifolia	Spanish-bayonet

VINES	
Trachelospermum jasminoides	confederate jasmine

GRASSES	
Cortaderia Selloana	pampas grass
Eremochloa ophiuroides	centipede grass

TRESCO ABBEY

Tresco Abbey House presides amid the plants established by Augustus Smith. The island was virtually barren when he arrived in 1834.

Tresco Island is one of the Isles of Scilly, set nearly thirty miles southwest of Land's End, the southwesternmost tip of England. Bathed by the warm waters and air of the Gulf Stream, Tresco enjoys a subtropical climate with average temperatures that range from forty-five degrees Fahrenheit on a cold day to sixty-three degrees on a warm one. Frost and extreme heat are rare, and the effects of occasional dry spells are offset by heavy seaside dews. However, the islands are blasted by winds. Storms from the Atlantic batter them regularly, saturating even the most inland sites with salt and barraging plants and people with what an islander once described as "scythes" of wind-blown sand.

Only coarse grass, bracken, and stunted buckthorn grow naturally on Tresco, and they were all that Augustus Smith found when he arrived in 1834, bearing a ninety-nine-year lease and the title of Lord Proprietor. Smith came as an experimenter: He was convinced that his program of self-help could convert the islands' impoverished residents to comfortable citizens. Socially, his project was somewhat successful; horticulturally, his accomplishment was nothing short of astonishing. Less than twenty years after moving to the barren island, Smith was overwhelmed by his success: "The garden is looking everywhere very gay, but immensely overgrown; I know not where I shall pack my treasures in the future," he wrote.

Tresco appealed to Smith because it had a lovely, sunny slope and a freshwater pond, but transforming the exposed site into a garden was a major project. He began humbly—with gorse, a stiffly branched, wind-resistant plant that provided shelter for the tender seedlings that were being nipped by wind as soon as they grew above the native grasses. Gradually, Smith planted full-scale windbreaks, using Monterey pines and cypresses, bishop pines (also native to California),

Above: *Plants from around the world shelter each other on Tresco's slopes.* **Center:** *The rugged rocks and rough seas that surround the Scilly Isles.* **Below:** *Palms and pines line the middle terrace walk.*

escallonia, and a New Zealand evergreen called *Metrosideros robustus*. On the lee side of the island he planted elms, sycamores, oaks, and poplars to provide shelter and cover for game.

Once the wind was buffered, Smith set about terracing the rocky slope and shaping distinct areas for planting. Two of the earliest features were a Long Walk, which displayed the many "rarities" that arrived from distant shores, and a rockery festooned with mesembryanthemums—a suc-

culent South African plant with brilliantly colored flowers that flourished in Tresco's climate.

Smith was an inveterate collector, and he found that his beds filled quickly, forcing him to expand the boundaries of his cultivated domain. He created an Upper Terrace that was to be the garden's chief feature—a three-hundred-yard-long walk at the top of the hill that commanded a spectacular view of the garden and the sea. An Aloe Walk led to a cypress rock-

Selected Plant List

("Spp.," the plural abreviation for species, indicates that several species within the genus are used.)

TREES

Acacia dealbata	silver wattle
Acacia melanoxylon	blackwood acacia
Chaemaecyparis Lawsoniana	Lawson's cypress
Cordyline australis	cabbage tree
Cupressus macrocarpa	Monterey cypress
Eucalyptus globulus	Tasmanian blue gum
Melaleuca linarifolia	flaxleaf paperbark
Metrosideros robustus	New Zealand Christmas tree
Pinus muricata	bishop pine
Pinus pinaster	maritime pine
Pinus pinea	Italian stone pine
Pinus radiata	Monterey pine
Populus alba	white poplar
Quercus ceris	turkey oak
Quercus ilex	holm oak
Quercus robur	English oak

SHRUBS

Aloe arborescens	tree aloe
Buddleia Davidii	butterfly bush
Callistemon citrinus	lemon bottlebrush
Camellia japonica	common camellia
Escallonia rubra	red escallonia
Fuchsia arborescens	tree fuchsia
Hebe spp.	hebes
Leptospermum scoparium	New Zealand tea tree
Myrtus communis	true myrtle
Pittosporum eugeniodes	New Zealand lemonwood
Pittosporum Tobira	Japanese pittosporum
Protea spp.	proteas
Rhododendron ponticum	ponticum rhododendron

ery, and sections called Higher Australia, Lower Australia, and Mexico harbored plants collected from those countries. At sea level, he established a forest full of Australian tree ferns; elsewhere he established an orchard and a vegetable garden. Ultimately, his garden covered twelve acres and included more than one hundred different types of plants.

Smith was an avid experimenter who enthusiastically received plants from travelers and constantly traded cuttings and seedlings with the Royal Botanic Garden at Kew in England. Like so many seaside gardeners, he seemed to enjoy pushing nature to her limits by growing plants native to regions far more southerly—South Africa and Australia, most notably. "More than usual survived last winter," he reported tersely in 1858. His successes far outweighed his losses, certainly, for his hillside was soon a sea of amaryllis, fuchsias, iris, ixia, sedums, and exotic succulents. Dracaenas and palms towered above beds full of cineraria, echium, and bromeliads; aralias, acacias and cassias filled the Australian gardens. His remarkable success was admired by tourists—a development that he found curious, for as

he was quick to acknowledge, neither the plan nor the plants were the least bit conventional. He went so far as to call the contents "rather curious," in fact. But something was always in bloom in the island garden, and the combination of exotic plants freely grown was rather a novelty. No doubt, the scale and exuberance of Tresco's naturalized plantings impressed many nineteenth-century English gardeners.

Smith's garden has flourished in spite of the storms and high winds that buffet Tresco. Trees that grow above the tops of the windbreaks are burned by the wind, and flowers are blasted in storms, but the plants always recover quickly—thanks, no doubt, to the mild climate. The Lord Proprietor's descendants have managed not only to maintain the garden but to expand the operation as well, taking full advantage of the weather by growing flowers for the London market. Narcissus are the mainstay (the paperwhite narcissus called "Soleil d' Or " was discovered growing wild on Tresco, incidentally); fields of amaryllis, lilies, hyacinths, tulips, freesias, anemones, wallflowers, and stock also flourish on the lee side of the island, com-

ing into blossom several weeks before fields elsewhere in England. The cut-flower experiment began in the 1880s, and early in the course of it, one of the garden's proprietors reported packing three-hundred dozen narcissus onto the daily boat that ferried between Tresco and the Covent Garden market. Tourism and cut flowers have helped keep Augustus Smith's garden going. It is hard to believe that he wouldn't be pleased with the picture of his garden—burgeoning on an island that was once so barren that not even a tree could grow there—supporting the place and the people that he sought to reform.

GROUND COVERS

Carpobrotus edulis	Hottentot fig
Erica cinerea	bell heather
Lampranthus spp.	ice plants

SUCCULENTS AND FLOWERING PLANTS

Aeonium arboreum	aeonium
Agave americana	century plant
Cistus spp.	rock roses
Crassula spp.	crassulas
Fuchsia fulgens	flame fuchsia
Iris kaempferi	Japanese iris
Kalanchoe spp.	kalanchoes
Opuntia spp.	prickly pears
Pelargonium spp.	geraniums
Phormium spp.	fiber lilies
Salvia patens	gentian salvia
Senecio cineraria	silver groundsel
Tropaeolum tuberosum	tuber nasturtium
Yucca aloifolia	Spanish-bayonet

Succulent rosettes of aeonium and blue-green agaves accent the hillside plantings.

PLIMPTON ASSOCIATES

Heathers, salt spray rose, and pines line a path overlooking the garden and the water.

Bearberry, Arctostaphylos Uva-ursi, *stretches glossy green sprays across a rock outcrop.*

A deck with a spectacular view is nestled into the rocky hillside.

This garden began as the rock-strewn backside of a large piece of land, with a stable and assorted outbuildings looking across a freshwater pond to Rhode Island Sound. When the stable was converted to a house, the owners wanted a long-term landscape plan that would help turn their narrow site toward the water, incorporating a pool, a new bedroom wing, a deck, and additional flowers and flowering shrubs that would tolerate the wind and salt spray.

The plan, launched almost ten years ago by landscape architects Susan and T.P. Plimpton, started with a deck along the waterside of the building that provides a striking water view and eases the dramatic drop in elevation that is typical behind barns but hardly suitable for a seaside house where easy indoor–outdoor movement is of the essence. The pool came next, nestled in the curve of a rock ledge where it lies comfortably protected from onshore winds. A fieldstone retaining wall shores up the ground between the two outcrops, creating a terrace for the

pool and eliminating the need for a perimeter fence. The solution is particularly effective visually, for it works like a "ha-ha"—the landscape device put to such good use by eighteenth-century English designers to keep animals out without interrupting the sweep of the scenery in the foreground.

The bank below the retaining wall spills down to the edge of the pond beneath loose masses of shrubbery. Indigenous species were chosen for this section of the garden because they would thrive, as well as look most familiar to neighbors across the water who had grown accustomed to their view of an uncultivated landscape. Along the top of the bank, clumps of bayberry, mountain laurel, and rhododendron provide color in winter and spring. Tupelos, red maples, and shadblows are set low on the slope where they can screen the view to the property without blocking it out. The trees are surrounded by shrubs that seem not to mind having their feet in moist ground and their leaves misted by salt-laden fog—clethra, fothergilla, aro-

nia, rhododendron, and viburnum.

Above the bank, the shallow end of the pool rests on the ledge, surrounded by a massive outcrop that provides enough privacy and protection to shelter a spa, complete with a jacuzzi and a waterfall that ties the two bodies of water into one. Simple bluestone paving and a pair of low steps flanking the spa create smooth horizontal lines, providing a striking contrast to the weathered rock. Stone steps leading from the pool terrace to the bedroom wing are rough-hewn granite, tied into a network of low retaining walls that seem to spill from the surrounding ledges. Mounds of Japanese roses and a veil of *Clematis paniculata* soften the lines of the deck as it rises nearly ten feet to the level of the ground floor.

Around the corner, Plimpton Associates carved a generously proportioned entry court out of the rocky hillside. The driveway ends in a parking space, and from there steps lead down to a bluestone walk that runs between a rose garden and a flower border arranged around a circle of grass. Here the planting is far more exuberant and the plan more formal, with bands of brightly colored annuals offset by the misty tones and textures of lavender, artemesia, and caryopteris. Both gardens are structured by low lines of boxwood and 'San Jose' juniper that hold their form and color when the surrounding flowers fade.

An entirely different sort of garden grows on the opposite side of the pool, along a path that leads to a high rock overlooking the pond. The plant palette is far more subdued in this situation, in deference to the surrounding scenery. From a distance, in fact, this garden is barely distinguishable from the adjacent drifts of native trees and shrubs. A red maple, shadblows, bayberries, and Japanese roses carry the line of the waterside plantings around the corner of the deck. But here, where foot traffic and observant eyes are expected, the ground is carpeted with a detailed tapestry of heathers woven in muted tones of greens, golds, pinks, and lavenders. Glossy green leaves and red berries of arctostaphylos offset the dusky hues of the heathers, creating a picture that is exquisite even in the bleak days of winter, when vestiges of roses and geraniums have disappeared and the seaside landscape is dominated by the monochromatic tones of weathered rock and dried grass.

Heathers provide rich color in winter.

Selected Plant List

("Spp.," the plural abbreviation for species, indicates that several species within the genus are used.)

TREES
Acer griseum	paperbark maple
Acer rubrum	red maple
Amelanchier canadensis	shadblow
Cornus kousa	Japanese dogwood
Magnolia virginiana	sweet bay
Malus hupehensis	tea crab apple
Nyssa sylvatica	tupelo
Pinus sylvestris cv. 'Watereri'	Waterer's Scotch pine
Pinus thunbergii	Japanese black pine
Tilia cordata 'Greenspire'	Greenspire littleleaf linden

ROSES
Hybrids	'Blanche'
	'Matterin'
	'Peace'
	'Seashell'
	'White Masterpiece'
Rosa hugonis	Father Hugo rose
Rosa rugosa	Japanese rose

SHRUBS
Hibiscus syriacus 'Blue Bird'	Blue Bird shrub althaea
Pinus mugo mughus	mugho pine
Potentilla 'Katherine Dykes'	Katherine Dykes cinquefoil
Rhododendron viscosum	swamp azalea
Rhododendron vaseyi	pinkshell azalea
Viburnum dentatum	arrowwood

PERENNIALS
Achillea 'Moonshine'	Moonshine yarrow
Artemesia spp.	artemisia
Astilbe spp.	astilbes
Hemerocallis 'Hyperion'	Hyperion day lily
Iris spp.	irises

ANNUALS
Antirrhinum spp.	snapdragons
Browallia spp.	browallia
Chrysanthemum frutescens	marguerite daisies
Nicotiana spp.	flowering tobaccos

GROUND COVERS
Calluna vulgaris	heather
Pachysandra terminalis	Japanese pachysandra
Paxistima canbyi	cliff green

VIZCAYA

Classical statues framed by blocks of sheared podocarpus and Australian pine line a path that overlooks Vizcaya's Italianate house and garden.

Vizcaya is an extraordinary place—a Renaissance palazzo set in Miami, Florida, overlooking a classic Italian garden where the rampant subtropical growth has been harnessed to form trim allees, hedges, and intricate parterres. Both house and garden were created in the early years of the twentieth century by James Deering, a well-traveled bachelor whose poor health necessitated warm winter weather. Deering's unusual choice of styles is attributable in part to the influ-

ence of his designer, Paul Chalfin, who had spent time in Rome as a fellow of the American Academy. The landscape architect, Diego Suarez, also had Italian connections: He had studied architecture in Florence and was involved in the restoration of Arthur Acton's garden at Villa La Pietra.

Today, Deering's winter retreat is a museum. The house opens east onto Biscayne Bay, its facades punctured by porches and pillared porticoes that make the most of cooling ocean breezes. To the

south, a series of sun-soaked terraces fall very gradually downhill to the level of the sea. On the inland side the garden is edged by a hammock—a section of native vegetation that Deering was determined to preserve—and on the waterside it is protected by the dense thickets of tangled mangroves that line the Florida coast. The surrounding vegetation completely encloses the garden, creating a seaside setting that is suitably scaled for the precise patterns of a formal garden.

*Above: Deering's stone barge serves as a sculptural bulwark, creating a protected harbor in front of Vizcaya's east facade. A viewing pavilion beyond nestles at the edge of the tangled mangroves that line Florida's coast. **Below:** In one of the peripheral garden rooms, water channeled through stone troughs surrounds an Italian fountain with strikingly Persian geometry.*

strained, just the opposite of subtropical vegetation, which are lush and exotic, with bold leaves and brightly colored flowers. Despite the unlikely match, Deering's artists managed to find a palette of subtropical plants that suited the Italian style. Native live oaks take the place of the holm oaks that shade Mediterranean gardens; Australian pine and podocarpus, though loose and billowy when grown naturally, are shearable, which makes them acceptable substitutes for the dense, dark cypresses that tower above Italian terraces. As in classical schemes, colorful flowers are contained in beds at Vizcaya. They are offset by the permanent planting there, which is predominantly green. Restraint is abandoned just once, in a corner of the garden close to the house, where masses of brightly colored bougainvillea spill over a stucco wall, offering exuberant evidence of the subtropical palette.

On the lower level, closer to the water, stands of mangrove and Australian pine shelter a series of smaller garden rooms—a fountain garden and a collection of roses, a maze planted with a native shrub called cocoplum, and an outdoor garden in the form of a theater, defined by walls of sheared silver buttonwood (*Conocarpus erectus* 'Sericeus').

Sculpture, stonework, and other classical features are scattered throughout the garden. Twin grottoes are set into the mount beneath a pair of stone staircases, their ceilings encrusted with Florida shells. On top of the mount, a summerhouse shaded by a grove of live oaks provides a cool retreat and overlook. Closer to the house, a *giardino segreto* (commonly called "secret garden") marks the corner between the south and east facades, sheltered by high walls that keep it separate (not actually secret, despite its common translation) from the main terraces. This is also a formal green garden, with a central bed edged by low jasmine hedges and standards of clipped eugenia. A border of mondo grass (*Ophiopogon japonicus*) softens the line between the walls and the stone paving; pale blue plumbago brimming from wall niches adds color.

The main terrace is structured by broad paths of finely crushed limestone gravel, packed earth, topiary trees, grass parterres, and patterned beds (called in French *broideries par terre*, that is, embroidery on the ground, or in English, parterres). An allee of clipped live oaks (*Quercus virginiana*) leads to a casino set high on top of a mount—an artificial device borrowed from ancient gardens to break the flatness of the Florida land-scape. Within the allee, a grassy island floats in a rectangular pool, highlighted by two rows of podocarpus clipped into rounded cones. To the side of this main terrace, a hedge of Australian pine (*Casuarina equisetifolia*) offsets an elevated statuary walk.

Vizcaya's unlikely combination of plan, plant palette, and prime waterfront setting gives the garden its unusual style. Classical gardens are characteristically re-

Malayan coconut palms line the walk to a pavilion once used for afternoon tea.

Beyond the *giardino segreto*, the east front of the house opens onto a view of Biscayne Bay. Here the mangrove tangle has been cleared, and the ground terraced down to a sea wall. The garden is reduced to the simplest, most seaworthy terms: sculpture, grass, packed earth, and keystone paving (a stone quarried in the Flordia Keys that is studded with coral and seashells). Deering's choice of sculpture is spectacular and eminently practical: He built a great stone barge and framed it with a pair of breakwaters that extend into the bay, creating a small protected harbor. The arms of the breakwaters are planted with Malayan coconut palms that echo the uprights of surrounding obelisks and

flagpoles. Both arms lead over stone bridges—the northern one to a place for landing boats, and the southern one to a teahouse perched at the edge of the mangroves. The tea pavilion is lined with sea-green latticework and paved with a black-and-white pattern that is particularly effective with the simple stretch of sea and horizon visible beyond. The massive barge has a classical balustrade, obelisks, sculpted masks, figures that symbolize the

sea, and long, low steps that run into the water, providing easy access to and from boats.

Here, at the water's edge, Deering and Vizcaya are at their best, as sea, sky, and sculpture come together to forge a unique seaside style. The design scheme is bold, subjecting nature to human designs and combining classical elements in a most original scheme that takes advantage of the Florida landscape.

Selected Plant List

("Spp.," the plural abbreviation for species, indicates that several species within the genus are used.)

TREES

Casuarina equisetifolia	Australian pine
Cocos nucifera	coconut palm
Conocarpus erectus var. 'Sericeus'	silver buttonwood
Ficus Benjamina	Benjamin fig
Phoenix reclinata	Senegal date palm
Quercus virginiana	live oak
Ravenala madagascariensis	traveler's tree
Sabal palmetto	sabal palm

SHRUBS

Chrysobalanus icaco	cocoplum
Codiaeum var. pictum	croton
Cycas revoluta	sago palm
Eugenia uniflora	Surinam cherry
Gardenia jasminoides	gardenia
Hibiscus rosa-sinensis	hibiscus
Ixora spp.	ixora
Murraya paniculata	orange-jessamine
Nerium Oleander	oleander
Podocarpus macrophyllus	yew podocarpus

VINES

Bouganvillea glabra	bouganvillea
Ficus pumila	creeping fig
Jasminum simplicifolium	jasmine

HERBACEOUS PLANTS

Asparagus sprengeri	asparagus fern
Ophiopogon japonicus	mondo grass
Peperomia obtusifolia	peperomia
Plumbago auriculata	plumbago
Thelypteris kunthii	marsh fern

DANIEL D. STEWART AND ASSOCIATES

Barely three years ago, this Long Island site was a flat, windswept field of goldenrod with only a few Japanese black pines and an unkempt privet hedge. Then came a contemporary house and plans that called for a pool, a tennis court, space for parking, and a place to grow flowers. The architect, Keith Kroeger, set the house high, at a grade where even the first-floor windows would offer splendid views of the beach and the Atlantic Ocean beyond. Then the landscape architects, Daniel Stewart and Associates, responded to the challenge of integrating the house with the site by pulling the undulating topography of the dunes up to the edge of the building. They built a new dune, in essence, perched the house on its crest, and nestled a series of outdoor rooms into its sandy slopes. Finally, they planted masses of new plants (nearly fifty thousand, they estimate) to secure the windblown sand and create a private, protected place from which people could enjoy the surrounding scenery.

The sloping ground on the ocean side of the house was terraced, with a pool set in a wooden deck. Clean lines and simple details provide a foreground that is appropriately understated, in deference to the ocean view. Benches that double as planting beds edge the deck, blocking wind and encouraging sand to build up on the surrounding dune rather than blowing into the pool. The planting is restrained, with geraniums in three compatible shades of pink and variegated vinca providing summer color. Shore and Andorra junipers (*J. conferta* and *J. horizontalis* var. 'Plumosa') assure interest in wintertime, and a row of upright Hanoki cypresses accent an adjacent wall.

From the deck, a long narrow boardwalk stretches out to the beach, through a section of the site that was planned and extensively planted to look almost entirely natural. The boardwalk crosses the trough between the dunes—an ecologically frag-

Alyssum, cleome, assorted flowers, and vegetables thrive in a cutting garden sunken below the gusty onshore winds. The gravel used throughout the site matches the color of the sand.

ile area where, to encourage stability, Daniel Stewart and Associates trapped and anchored windblown sand with masses of pioneer plants. Their effort began with the construction of a snow fence—a step that required the local coastal commission's approval. Approximately four inches of sand collected in the first year, establishing a good base for the new dune. With that, a dense cover of beach grass and native shrubs could be established and counted on to carry on the role of holding the shifting sand in place. Bayberries, salt spray roses, inkberry, clethra, and highbush blueberries form shrubby thickets; shore juniper and mugho pine hug the ground. Bearberry cotoneaster (*Cotoneaster dammeri*) takes the place of ordinary bearberry (*Archtostaphylos Uva-ursi*)—a native ground cover that the landscape architects admire but found extremely difficult to locate. Clumps

of ornamental grasses accent the beach grass, providing interest without disrupting the harmony of the naturalized landscape.

The naturalized zone extends across the oceanfront of the site and wraps around the house, stretching inland along the property lines. On the far side of the pool deck, the newly planted thicket hugs the edge of a sunken cutting garden. Japanese black pines and a mound of elaeagnus provide additional protection, shielding flowers and herbs from the salt-laced wind. Within the garden, raised beds set in gravel paths echo the lines of the pool deck. The beds and retaining walls are built of railroad ties that have been stained to match the sand-colored deck; each bed is raised to a height of twenty-four inches, providing good footing for plants and easy

maintenance for people. Clumps of day lilies, cleome, snapdragons, and baby's breath tower above mats of white and purple allyssum; gladiolus, dahlias, herbs, strawberries, and a few vegetables find comfortable footing alongside.

On the lee side of the house, the landscape has a distinctly different character. Here, the designers decided to take advantage of the sloping ground by building a tennis court into the backside of the dune. The court is surrounded by a retaining wall and perimeter stands of salt-tolerant trees—red cedars, black pines, and American holly, primarily. A veil of silverfleece vine softens the railroad tie wall in summer, reducing glare and reflected heat. The evergreen screen is supplemented by a few sycamores (*Platanus*

*Above: Mugho pines and inkberry around a pavilion that provides shade for tennis players and spectators. **Below:** A formal entrance with annuals, privet, and pines.*

Selected Plant List

("Spp.," the plural abbreviation for species, indicates that several species within the genus are used.)

TREES
Amelanchier canadensis	shadblow
Cercis canadensis	redbud
Cryptomeria japonica	cryptomeria
Elaeagnus angustifolia	Russian olive
Ilex opaca	American holly
Juniperus virginiana	eastern red cedar
Pinus thunbergi	Japanese black pine

SHRUBS
Clethra alnifolia	summersweet
Cotoneaster dammeri	bearberry cotoneaster
Cytisus praecox	warminster broom
Ilex glabra	inkberry
Juniperus conferta	shore juniper
Myrica pennsylvanica	bayberry
Prunus maritima	beach plum
Rhus aromatica	fragrant sumac
Rosa rugosa	salt spray rose
Vaccinum corymbosum	highbush blueberry

GROUND COVERS
Ammophilia breviligulata	American beach grass
Euonymous fortunei coloratus	wintercreeper

Wooden benches surround the pool deck, retaining beds of native shrubs that include bayberry, beachplum, inkberry, and salt spray rose. Boxes of geraniums add color to the restrained palette.

An unusual allee of specimen Japanese black pines lines the entrance drive.

PERENNIALS	
Achillea millefolium	yarrow
Asclepias tuberosa	butterfly milkweed
Gypsophilia paniculata	baby's breath
Hemerocallis hybrids	day lilies
Iberis sempervirens	candytuft
Iris kaempferi	Japanese iris
Iris siberica	Siberian iris
Lavandula officinalis	lavender
Lupinus hybrids	lupine
Lythrum salicaria	loosestrife
Paeonia officinalis	peony
Phlox paniculata	garden phlox
Scabiosa caucasia	pincushion flower

ANNUALS	
Agapanthus spp.	agapanthus
Antirrhinum spp.	snapdragons
Chrysanthemum frutescens	marguerite daisies
Dahlia spp.	dahlias
Gladiolus spp.	gladiolus
Polianthes tuberosa	tuberose
Zantedeschia aetheopica	calla lily

occidentalis) (one of the "safest" deciduous trees to use so close to the sea, according to associate Donald Walsh) and a covered pavilion.

On the far side of the driveway, the naturalized zone curls around the house and gradually tapers down to a cluster of trees and shrubs that screens the site from the street. Despite the informal perimeters, however, this section of the landscape is dominated by an arrow-straight allee of Japanese black pines that leads from the street to the front door. The formality of this allee will be tempered over time, as the pines assume their characteristically irregular silhouettes; but the crisp lines of the granite-edged driveway and entry court and the striking plantings—including white-stemmed birch and a handsome combination of clipped Japanese holly and variegated euonymous—will always serve as a link to the formality of the street and the adjacent properties, and as a compelling contrast to the seaside scenery that unfolds around the corner.

RESOURCES

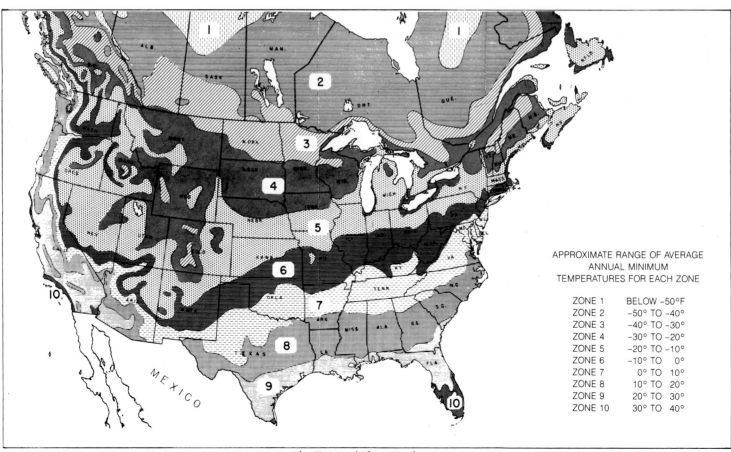

APPROXIMATE RANGE OF AVERAGE
ANNUAL MINIMUM
TEMPERATURES FOR EACH ZONE

ZONE 1	BELOW –50°F
ZONE 2	–50° TO –40°
ZONE 3	–40° TO –30°
ZONE 4	–30° TO –20°
ZONE 5	–20° TO –10°
ZONE 6	–10° TO 0°
ZONE 7	0° TO 10°
ZONE 8	10° TO 20°
ZONE 9	20° TO 30°
ZONE 10	30° TO 40°

The Zones of Plant Hardiness

SELECTED PLANT LIST

• Due to extreme variations in seaside climates and microclimates, you should consult local horticulturists, contractors, growers, or nurserymen before making final decisions about plants.
• "Spp." is the plural abbreviation for species. It refers here to the recommendation of different species within the named genus.
• Entries for plant names are arranged in the following order: scientific name, common name, hardiness zone (if applicable), description.

ANNUAL FLOWERS

Calendula officinalis
pot marigold
Orange, daisylike flowers

Chrysanthemum frutescens
marguerite
Classic white daisies with yellow centers

Cineraria maritima
cineraria
Blue, pink, or white flowers

Cleome Hasslerana
spider flower
Round heads of pink or white flowers, self-seeds

Coreopsis spp.
coreopsis
Yellow daisylike flowers

Cosmos spp.
cosmos
Pink, white, or orange flowers, finely cut foliage

Eschscholtzia californica
California poppy
Orange and yellow flowers, fine grayish foliage

Felicia amelloides
blue Felicia
Blue daisylike flowers, low growing

Fuchsia spp.
fuchsias
Hanging bell-like flowers, red, purple, deep pink, and white

Helianthus spp.
sunflowers
Large yellow flowers on upright stalks

Lantana spp.
lantana
Flowers open yellow, fade to orange and red, low growing

Lathyrus odoratus
sweet pea
Fragrant pastel-colored flowers on climbing vine

Nicotiana spp.
flowering tobaccos
Pink, red, or white flowers

Nigella damascena
love-in-a-mist
Blue flowers, lacy foliage

Petunia spp.
petunias
Multicolored flowers

Portulaca spp.
moss roses
Multicolored flowers, fleshy leaves, low growing

Senecio cineraria
silver groundsel
Silvery leaves

Tagetes spp.
marigolds
Yellow or orange flowers

Tropaeolum spp.
nasturtiums
Red, orange, or yellow flowers, round leaves, low growing

Verbena spp.
vervains
Heads of red, pink, white, blue, and purple flowers, low growing

Zinnia spp.
zinnias
Red, orange, pink, yellow flowers, upright

GRASSES
Beach and Ornamental Grasses

Ammophila breviligulata
American beach grass
Zone 5

Cortaderia Selloana
pampas grass
Zone 8
Large clumps, with graceful white plumes

Festuca ovina var. 'glauca'
blue fescue
Zone 4
Fine light blue foliage, grows in tufts

Miscanthus sinensis
eulalia grass
Zone 4
Tall grass, feathery plumes

Molina spp.
molinia grass
Zones 4–9
Dense tufts, persistent flower spikes

Panicum spp.
panicgrass
Zones 5–10

Pennisetum alopecuroides
rose fountain grass
Zone 7
Thin leaves, pink flower spikes mid- and late summer

Uniola panicolata
sea oats
Zone 6

Lawn Grasses

Cynodon Dactylon
Bermuda grass
Southern, browns in cold weather

Eremochloa ophiuroides
centipede grass
Southern, dense, coarsely textured, good on poor soils

Festuca spp.
fescues
Northern, wiry texture, often mixed with Kentucky bluegrass

Poa pratensis
'Merion' bluegrass
Northern, dense, and low growing

Stenotaphrum secundatum
St. Augustine grass
Southern, coarsely textured

Zoysia japonica
zoysia
Southern, finely textured, browns in winter

GROUND COVERS

Abronia umbellata
prostrate sand verbena
Zone 8
Pink flowers

Arcostaphylos Uva-ursi
bearberry
Zone 2
Evergreen foliage, bronze in fall,
red berries

Atriplex semibaccata
creeping saltbush
Zone 8
Mats of finely textured gray-green
foliage

Calluna vulgaris
heather
Zone 4
White, pink or red flower spikes
in summer, evergreen foliage

Carpobrotus edulis
Hottentot fig
Zone 10
Purple or pink flowers, succulent
foliage

Cerastostigma plumbaginoides
blue plumbago
Zones 5–6
Tufts of glossy foliage reddish in
fall, almost evergreen, long-lasting
deep blue flowers, late summer

Cotoneaster Dammeri
bearberry cotoneaster
Zones 5–6
Evergreen leaves, bright red fruits

Cotoneaster horizontalis
rock cotoneaster
Zone 4
Semi-evergreen, red berries,
horizontal branching

Delosperma 'Alba'
white trailing ice plant
Zone 9
Succulent leaves, small white
flowers

Erica carnea
spring heath
Zone 5
Needlelike evergreen leaves,
white or pink flowers bloom
between January and May

Fragaria chiloensis
beach strawberry
Zones 4–5
Glossy leaves, reddish in
winter, white spring flowers
followed by small seedy
fruit attractive to birds

Hypericum calycinum
Aaron's-beard, Saint-John's-wort
Zone 6
Yellow summer flowers, purplish
fall color

Iberis sempervirens
edging candytuft
Zone 3
Flat clusters of white flowers,
long lasting,
semi-evergreen leaves

Ipomoea spp.
morning glories
Zones 5–10
Blue or pink flowers, twining habit

Juniperus conferta
shore juniper
Zone 5
Evergreen, bluish green foliage

Juniperus horizontalis
creeping juniper
Zone 2
Evergreen, many varieties

Liriope spp.
lily-turfs
Zones 4–6
Dark green grassy leaves,
small spikes of blue
flowers, late summer

Opuntia compressa
prickly pear
Zone 6
Cactus with yellow flowers,
purplish fruit

Osteospermum fruticosum
trailing African daisy
Zone 9
Purplish white daisylike flowers,
November to March, spreads
rapidly

Paxistima Canbyi
cliff green
Zone 5
Low ericaceous evergreen,
bronze in fall; small white flowers

Phlox subulata
moss pink
Zones 2–3
Pink or white spring flowers,
semi- evergreen foliage, matted
growth

Rosa wichuriana
memorial rose
Zone 5
Small white flowers, late summer,
semi-evergreen foliage

HERBACEOUS PLANTS

Achillea spp.
yarrow
Zones 2–7
Fernlike foliage, flat heads of
yellow or white flowers

Althaea rosea
hollyhock
Spires of red, pink, yellow,
or white flowers,
single blossoms preferable

Alyssum saxatile
gold dust
Zone 4
Low growing, gray-leaved plant
with bright yellow spring flowers

Arabis spp.
rock cresses
Zones 3–7
Low growing, small spring flowers

Armeria maritima
common thrift
Zone 3
Rounded heads of pink
flowers, late spring, grasslike
evergreen leaves

Artemesia stellerana
dusty-miller
Zones 2–3
Silvery foliage

Campanula carpatica
Carpathian bellflower
Zone 3
Blue bell-like flowers,
early summer

Cerastium tomentosum
snow-in-summer
Zones 2-3
Silvery foliage, evergreen, white
spring flowers

Chrysanthemum spp.
daisies
Zones 2–10
Daisylike flowers, many species
and varieties available

Delphinium spp.
delphinium hybrids
Zones 2–3
Spikes of blue flowers

Dianthus spp.
pinks
Zones 2–5
Grasslike evergreen leaves,
fragrant carnationlike flowers

Digitalis spp.
foxglove
Zones 3–4
Spikes of pastel-colored flowers,
spring, biennial

Echinops spp.
globe thistle
Zone 3
Rounded heads of blue flowers,
gray thistly leaves

Erigeron spp.
fleabanes
Zones 2–9
White to purple daisylike flowers

Eryngium maritimum
sea holly
Zone 5
Low growing thistlelike leaves,
blue flowers

Euryops Evansii
euryops
Zone 9
Daisylike flowers, long blooming
season

Gypsophila spp.
baby's breath
Zones 2–3
Airy masses of tiny white flowers.

Hemerocallis spp.
day lilies
Zones 2–7
Orange, pink, yellow midsummer
flowers

Heuchera sanguinea
coral bells
Zone 3
Delicate spikes of red flowers

Hibiscus moscheutos
swamp rose mallow
Zone 5
Large red, pink, or white flowers,
late summer

Lavandula officinalis
lavender
Zone 5
Evergreen gray foliage, spikes of
blue, white, or pink flowers

Lythrum salicaria
loosestrife
Zone 3
Spikes of purplish red flowers,
June through September

Paeonia spp.
peonies
Zone 3
Large fragrant spring flowers in
pink, white, red, or yellow
flowers, handsome foliage

Phlox paniculata
garden phlox
Zone 4
Tall heads of pink or white
fragrant flowers, midsummer
to late summer

Phormium tenax
New Zealand flax
Zone 9
Long leathery leaves

Santolina chamaecyparissus
lavender cotton
Zones 6–7
Silver-leaved evergreen, yellow
flowers

Sedum spectabile
showy sedum
Zone 3
Fleshy gray-green leaves, flat
clusters of pink flowers,
long lasting

SHRUBS

Acacia longifolia var. floribunda
gossamer Sydney acacia
Zone 10
Flowering, evergreen,
fast growing

Baccharis halimifolia
groundselbush
Zone 4
White fruit, separate sexes

Buddleia Davidii
butterfly bush
Zone 5
Colorful flower spikes, late
summer, dies to ground in winter

Camellia japonica
common camellia
Zone 7
Evergreen, flowers late fall
through early spring

Carissa grandiflora
natal plum
Zone 9
Evergreen, fragrant white
flowers, shearable

Caryopteris x clandonensis
hybrid bluebeard
Zone 5
Silvery foliage, blue flowers,
late summer

Ceanothus x delilianus
California lilac
Zone 7
Evergreen, blue flowers in spring

Chaenomeles speciosa
flowering quince
Zone 4
Flowers white, pink, red, orange;
thorny, shearable

Cistus spp.
rock roses
Zone 7
Multicolored flowers, evergreen

Clethra alnifolia
summersweet
Zone 3
Fragrant midsummer flowers,
white or pink, yellow and orange
fall foliage

Coccoloba Uvifera
sea grape
Zone 10
Large leathery leaves, edible fruit

Codiaeum var. pictum
croton
Zone 10
Multicolored evergreen leaves

Comptonia peregrina
sweetfern
Zone 2
Aromatic fernlike foliage

Coprosma repens
mirror plant
Zone 9
Evergreen, glossy leaves, small
orange fruit

Cornus sericea
red osier dogwood
Zone 2
Red-stemmed shrub with white
flowers and fruits

Corylus americana
American filbert
Zone 4
Early spring catkins, edible nuts

Cotoneaster spp.
cotoneasters
Zones 4–6
Large group of spreading shrubs
with glossy leaves, red berries

Cytisus spp.
broom
Zones 5–9
Yellow pealike flowers

Elaeagnus spp.
elaeagnus
Zones 2–7
Silvery foliage, colorful fruit

Escallonia spp.
escallonias
Zones 7–8
Red or white summer flowers,
evergreen foliage

Euonymus japonica
spindle tree
Zone 7
Glossy evergreen foliage,
compact habit

Forsythia spp.
forsythia
Zone 4
Fast-growing shrub with brilliant
yellow flowers in early spring,
before leaves

Genista spp.
broom
Zones 2–7
Yellow pealike flowers

Hamamelis mollis
Chinese witch hazel
Zone 5
Fragrant yellow flowers,
very early spring

Hebe spp.
hebes
Zones 5–10
White to pink flowers, finely
textured evergreen foliage

Hibiscus syriacus
shrub althaea
Zone 5
Multicolored flowers, late summer

Hydrangea macrophylla
flowering hydrangea
Zones 5–6
Large globes of blue or pink
flowers, midsummer

Ilex glabra
inkberry
Zone 3
Evergreen foliage, black berries

Ilex vomitoria
yaupon holly
Zone 7
Evergreen, profuse red fruits,
shearable

Juniperus chinensis cv.'Pfitzeriana'
Pfitzer's juniper
Zone 4
Evergreen, spreading

Juniperus communis
common juniper
Zone 2
Evergreen, many cultivars
available

Leptospermum laevigatum
Australian tea tree
Zone 9
White or red spring flowers,
small evergreen leaves

Lonicera nitida
box honeysuckle
Zone 7
Fragrant white flowers, blue fruits

Myrica pennsylvanica
bayberry
Zone 2
Semi-evergreen leaves, waxy
blue berries

Nerium Oleander
oleander
Zones 7–8
White, red, pink, or yellow
flowers bloom all summer,
evergreen foliage

Pinus Mugo mughus
mugho pine
Zone 2
Dwarf pine, forming a
dense mound

Pittosporum Tobira
Japanese pittosporum
Zone 8
Evergreen leaves, fragrant flowers

Podocarpus macrophyllus
yew podocarpus
Zone 7
Evergreen foliage, similar to
yew but longer

Potentilla fruticosa
bush cinquefoil
Zone 2
Yellow or white flowers,
midsummer to late summer, many
varieties available

Prunus maritima
beach plum
Zone 3
Edible fruit, white spring flowers

Rhamnus spp.
buckthorns
Zones 2–7
Deciduous and evergreen
shrubs, small black berries
attractive to birds

Rhododendron Vaseyi
pinkshell azalea
Zone 4
Deciduous, with red leaves
in tall, rosy flowers in midspring
before leaves appear

Rhododendron viscosum
swamp azalea
Zone 3
Fragrant white spring flowers,
deciduous foliage

Rhus spp.
sumacs
Zones 2–9
Orange and red fall foliage,
compound leaves

Rosa rugosa
salt spray rose
Zone 2
Pink or white flowers,
glossy green leaves,
large orangy red hips

Rosa virginiana
Virginia rose
Zone 3
Single pink flowers, red hips,
red fall foliage,
red twigs in winter

Sambucus canadensis
American elder
Zone 3
Flat clusters of white flowers
followed by edible black berries,
attractive to birds

Skimmia japonica
Japanese skimmia
Zone 7
Evergreen leaves,
white flowers, red berries,
sexes separate

Spiraea spp.
spireas
Zones 3–7
Sturdy shrubs with white,
pink, or red flowers

Syringa vulgaris
common lilac
Zone 3
Fragrant white or lavender spring
flowers

Tamarix parvifloria
small-flowered tamarisk
Zone 4
Small pink flowers, late spring,
heathlike foliage

Taxus cuspidata
Japanese yew
Zone 4
Dark green evergreen, shearable,
many varieties available

Vaccinium corymbosum
highbush blueberry
Zone 3
Edible fruit, white heathlike
flowers, brilliant fall color

Viburnum spp.
viburnums, snowballs
Zones 2–9
Flowering shrubs, many fragrant,
with ornamental fruit and
good fall color

Yucca aloifolia
Spanish-bayonet
Zone 8
Stiff-leaved rosette, spike of white
bell-like flowers, late summer

TREES

Acer griseum
paperbark maple
Zone 5
Small tree with compound leaves,
exfoliating bark

Acer platanoides
Norway maple
Zone 3
Yellow leaves in fall, quick growing

Acer pseudoplatanus
sycamore maple
Zone 5
No fall color, but varieties with
colored leaves available

Aesculus Hippocastanum
horse chestnut
Zone 3
Large leaves, white flowers,
creates dense shade

Ailanthus altissima
tree-of-heaven
Zone 4
Compound leaves, valuable where
almost nothing else will grow

Albizia julibrissin
silk tree
Zone 7
Pink powder-puff flowers, blooms
young

Amelanchier spp.
shadblow
Zone 4
White flowers, early spring; red
fruit attractive to birds; red and
yellow fall foliage

Casuarina equisetifolia
Australian pine
Zone 9
Quick-growing, vulnerable to
storm damage, shearable

Catalpa speciosa
western catalpa
Zone 4
White flowers, late June

Cedrus atlantica cv. 'Glauca'
blue atlas cedar
Zone 6
Specimen evergreen, becomes
very large

Cedrus Deodara
deodar cedar
Zone 7
Specimen evergreen

Chamaecyparis spp.
false cypress
Zones 3–5
Evergreen genus, including trees
and shrubs

Cocos nucifera
coconut palm
Zone 10
The classic beach palm, with
slender, leaning trunk, edible
coconuts

Cordyline australis
cabbage tree
Zone 10
Very colorful foliage

Crataegus spp.
hawthorns
Zone 4
Pink or white spring flowers, finely
textured foliage, thorns

Cryptomeria japonica
Japanese cedar
Zone 5
Specimen evergreen

Cupressus macrocarpa
Monterey cypress
Zone 7
Evergreen, shearable, cragged,
windswept silhouette

Eriobotrya japonica
loquat
Zone 7
Large evergreen leaves, fragrant
flowers, edible fruit

Eucalpytus spp.
gum trees
Zones 8–10
Fast-growing evergreen trees with
interesting bark, aromatic foliage,
ornamental flowers and seeds

Feijoa Sellowiana
pineapple guava
Zone 10
Evergreen with silvery leaves,
purplish flowers, edible fruit

Fagus spp.
beeches
Zones 3–4
Large, slow-growing deciduous
trees, often used as specimens

Ficus spp.
banyans
Zones 6–10
Tropical trees, primarily
evergreen, many very large

Gleditsia triacanthos
honey locust
Zone 3
Fast-growing tree with lacy
leaves that cast light shade

Hippophae rhamnoides
sea buckthorn
Zone 3
Willowlike gray leaves,
orange berries

Ilex opaca
American holly
Zone 5
Evergreen, red berries, sexes
separate

Juniperus virginiana
eastern red cedar
Zone 2
Columnar evergreen,
bluish berries

Laurus nobilis
laurel
Zone 7
Evergreen, shearable, often
trained as standards

Ligustrum ovalifolium
Californian privet
Zone 5
Semideciduous, fragrant flowers,
black berries

Magnolia grandiflora
southern magnolia
Zone 7
Specimen evergreen, large
leaves, large fragrant flowers

Magnolia virginiana
sweet bay magnolia
Zone 5
Very fragrant flowers,
early summer

Malus spp.
crab apples
Zones 2–4
Large genus with spring flowers,
fall fruit

Melaleuca quinquenervia
paperbark tree
Zone 10
Shredding bark, picturesque
branching, gray-green leaves,
flowers, ornamental woody fruit,
fast growing

Nyssa sylvatica
black tupelo
Zone 4
Brilliant red foliage in fall

Olea europaea
common olive
Zone 9
Silvery foliage

Oxydendrum arboreum
sourwood
Zone 5
Late summer flowers, glossy
leaves, brilliant red in fall

Picea glauca
white spruce
Zone 2
Pyramidal evergreen

Pinus pinea
Italian stone pine
Zone 9
Specimen pine, picturesque growth
habit, edible nuts

Pinus radiata
Monterey pine
Zone 7
Rugged evergreen

Pinus rigida
pitch pine
Zone 4
Scrub tree, picturesque wnen older

Pinus sylvestris
Scotch pine
Zone 2
Bluish green needles, shredding
orange bark

Pinus Thunbergii
Japanese black pine
Zone 4
Fast growing, picturesque
silhouette develops with age

Platanus acerifolia
London plane tree
Zone 5
Exfoliating bark, decorative
seedpods

Populus alba
white poplar
Zone 3
Leaves white below, shimmer in
wind

Prunus serotina
black cherry
Zone 3
Profuse white flowers, red fruit,
graceful drooping branches

Prunus virginiana
choke cherry
Zone 2
Small white flowers, black fruits
edible and attractive to birds

Pyrus calleryana
callery pear
Zone 5
Clusters of white flowers bloom
before leaves unfold, glossy red
foliage in fall

Quercus alba
white oak
Zone 4
Purplish red fall color,
slow growing

Quercus ilex
holm oak
Zone 9
Evergreen hollylike leaves,
spreading crown

Quercus palustris
pin oak
Zone 4
Red fall foliage, pyramidal
silhouette

Robinia pseudoacacia
black locust
Zone 3
Finely textured pinnate leaves,
fragrant flowers, looks particularly
well grown in groves

Roystonea regia
Cuban royal palm
Zone 10
One of most elegant palms,
gracefully tapering trunk

Sabal palmito
sabal palmetto
Zone 8
Fanlike leaves

Salix alba
white willow
Zone 2
Upright, with open crown, several varieties available

Sassafras albidum
sassafras
Zone 4
Red and orange fall foliage, irregular leaves

Schinus molle
California pepper tree
Zone 9
Fast-growing tree with fine leaves, red fruit, weeping habit

Sciadopitys verticillata
umbrella pine
Zone 5
Specimen evergreen

Sorbus aucuparia
European mountain ash
Zone 2
Clusters of white flowers followed by decorative reddish orange fruit, pinnate leaves reddish in fall

Styrax japonicus
Japanese snowbell
Zone 5
Small specimen with white flowers below branches in spring

Tilia cordata
littleleaf linden
Zone 3
Tight crown, fragrant flowers, slow growing

Ulmus parvifolia
Chinese elm
Zone 5
Exfoliating bark, small leaves reddish in fall

Umbellularia californica
California laurel
Zone 7
Broad-leaved evergreen with fragrant leaves

VINES

Ampelopsis brevipedunculata
porcelain vine
Zone 3
Vigorous vine with grapelike leaves, lovely blue, white, and lavender berries in fall

Bougainvillea glabra
bougainvillea
Zone 10
Pink, purple, or yellow summer flowers

Campsis radicans
trumpet vine
Zone 4
Orange trumpetlike flowers, midsummer

Celastrus spp.
bittersweets
Zones 2–5
Orange berries, fall

Clematis paniculata
sweet autumn clematis
Zone 5
Fragrant white flowers, late summer, interesting seeds

Gelsemium sempervirens
evening trumpet flower
Zone 7
Fragrant yellow spring flowers

Hydrangea peteolaris
climbing hydrangea
Zone 4
Glossy leaves, white summer flowers

Lathryus latifolius
perennial pea
Zone 3
Pink sweet pealike flowers

Lonicera spp.
honeysuckles
Zones 3–7
Fragrant flowers, ornamental fruits

Parthenocissus tricuspidata
Boston ivy
Zone 4
Clinging vine with red fall foliage, blue fruit

Passiflora spp.
passionflowers
Zones 6–8
Fast-growing vines with fascinating flowers, fruit

Rosa spp.
rambling and climbing roses
Zones 2–7
Many varieties, all need support

Smilax glauca
catbrier
Zone 5
Partially evergreen foliage, prickly stems

Solandra maxima
cup-of-gold vine
Zone 10
Fragrant yellow flowers, evergreen foliage

Tecomaria capensis
Cape honeysuckle
Zone 9
Clusters of orange flowers, evergreen leaves

Trachelospermum jasminoides
confederate jasmine
Zone 9
Clusters of fragrant white flowers, early summer, evergreen foliage

Vitis labrusca
fox grape
Zone 5
Rampant grower with edible fruit

Wisteria sinensis
Chinese wisteria
Zone 5
Clusters of lavender or white fragrant flowers, ornamental seedpods

RETAIL NURSERIES

(These nurseries either carry or specialize in plants suitable for seaside gardens.)

ATLANTIC NURSERY
250 Atlantic Avenue
Freeport, New York 11520

BERKELEY HORTICULTURAL NURSERY
1310 McGee Avenue
Berkeley, California 94703

CURRIES NURSERY
909 South Staples
Corpus Christi, Texas 78404

EAST MARSH NURSERY, INC.
7100 Hillsborough Canal Road
Pompano Beach, Florida 33067

EASTERN SHORE NURSERIES
Box 743, Route 331
Easton, Maryland 21601

ALLEN C. HASKELL
787 Shawmut Avenue
New Bedford, Massachusetts 02746
(evergreens, ground covers, perennials, standards)

TURK HESSELUND NURSERY
1255 Coast Village Road
Santa Barbara, California 93108
(salt-tolerant plants)

HENRY LEUTHARDT
NURSERIES, INC.
Montauk Highway
Box 666
East Moriches, New York 11940
(espalier, dwarf and semidwarf fruit trees)

MERRIHEW NURSERY
1426 Montana Avenue
Santa Monica, California 90403

NATIVE TREE NURSERY
17250 Southwest 232nd Street
Goulds, Florida 33170

STORM NURSERY
Box 889
Premont, Texas 78375

THE THEODORE PAYNE
FOUNDATION FOR
WILDFLOWERS AND
NATIVE PLANTS
10459 Tuxford Street
Sun Valley, California 91352

MARTIN VIETTE NURSERIES
Route 25A
East Norwich, New York 11732
(trees, shrubs, perennials, wildflowers)

WESTERN HILLS NURSERY
16250 Coleman Valley Road
Occidental, California 95465

WOODLANDERS INC.
1128 Colleton Avenue
Aiken, South Carolina 29801
(plants native to the Southern coastal plain)

YERBA BUENA NURSERY
19500 Skyline Boulevard
Woodside, California 94062
(California natives, exotic ferns)

DESIGNERS

MARK BERRY
1294 Mar Vista
Pasadena, California 91104

JOHN BROOKES
Clock House Denmans
Fontwell nr. Arundel
Sussex BN180SU
England

PAMELA BURTON
2324½ Michigan Avenue
Santa Monica, California 90404

A.E. BYE
523 East Putnam Avenue
Greenwich, Connecticut 06830

ENGEL/GGP
204 West 27th Street
New York, New York 10001

ROBERT FLETCHER
11100 Chalon Road
Los Angeles, California 90049

FORD, POWELL & CARSON, INC.
1138 East Commerce Street
San Antonio, Texas 78205

ISABELLE C. GREENE &
ASSOCIATES
34 East Sola
Santa Barbara, California 93101

INNOCENTI & WEBEL
The Studio
Box 260
Greenvale, New York 11548

ALICE IREYS
45 Willow Street
Brooklyn, New York 11201

DIANE McGUIRE
209 Bol Walker Hall
School of Architecture
University of Arkansas
Fayetteville, Arkansas 72701

OEHME, VAN SWEDEN
& ASSOCIATES
2813 North Street, Northwest
Washington, D.C. 20007

EDWARD PINCKNEY/
ASSOCIATES, LTD.
Box 5339
Hilton Head Island,
South Carolina 29928

JONATHAN PLANT
3540 Wilkonson Lane
Lafayette, California 94549

PLIMPTON ASSOCIATES
Pojac Point
North Kingston, Rhode Island
02852

NANCY GOSLEE POWER
615 20th Street
Santa Monica, California 90402

LISA STAMM
67 Manantic Road
Shelter Island, New York 11965

DANIEL D. STEWART
& ASSOCIATES
237 West 18th Street
New York, New York 10011

EDWARD D. STONE
AND ASSOCIATES
1512 East Broward Boulevard
Suite 110
Fort Lauderdale, Florida 33301

EMMET L. WEMPLE
& ASSOCIATES
2503 West Seventh Street
Los Angeles, California 90057

PHILIP WINSLOW
8 West 40th Street
New York, New York 10018

ZION & BREEN
P.O. Box 34
Imlaystown, New Jersey 08562

REFERENCES FOR FURTHER READING

Bardswell, Frances A. *Seacoast Gardens and Gardening.* London: Sherratt & Hughes, 1908.

Foley, Daniel J. *Gardening by the Sea.* Orleans, Mass.: Parnassus Imprints, 1965.

Lindley, Kevin. *Seaside Architecture.* London: Hugh Evelyn, 1973.

Lounsberry, Alice. *Gardens Near the Sea.* New York: Frederick A. Stokes Comp., 1910.

Martineau, Mrs. Philip. *Gardening in Sunny Lands: The Riviera, California, Australia.* London: Richard Cobden-Sanderson, 1924.

Martineau, Mrs. Philip. *The Secrets of Many Gardens.* London: Williams & Northgate, 1924.

Menninger, Edwin A. *Seaside Plants of the World.* New York: Hearthside Press, Inc., 1964.

Schmidt, R. Marilyn. *Gardening on the Eastern Shore.* Barnegat Light, N.J.: Barnegat Light Press, 1983.

Sheperd, F.W. *Gardening by the Sea.* London: The Royal Horticultural Society, 1982.

Thaxter, Celia. *An Island Garden.* Boston: Houghton Mifflin & Co., 1895.

GLOSSARY

Acid. Indicates a low pH (less than 7); typical of soils in areas with moderate to heavy rain. Most plants will grow in slightly acid soil, which gardeners also call "sour" soil.

Alkaline. Indicates a high pH (greater than 7); typical of soils developed from limestone rock. Alkaline soil is occasionally referred to as "sweet," and is typical in sandy seaside situations.

Annual. A plant that completes its life cycle in one year.

Biennial. A plant that completes its life cycle in two years.

Deciduous. Describes a plant's characteristic of dropping leaves in autumn.

Exotic. A plant that is indigenous to a different part of the world from where it is growing.

Giardino segreto. A garden within a garden, featured often in Italian renaissance plans; a place set apart or separate, where different design themes can be pursued without detracting from the quality of the principal garden.

Girdle. A band of bark removed from the circumference of a tree, usually resulting in the death of the tree. The process, referred to as girdling, is also called "cutting the cambium," the tissue through which the tree's nutrients are transported.

Ha-ha. A type of retaining wall, specially designed to be invisible from the ground on the uphill side. A device used frequently by eighteenth-century landscape designers to keep foraging animals on the downhill side of a sloping lawn while preserving the integrity of the view across a grassy landscape.

Halophyte. A plant that is capable of surviving in unusually alkaline or saline soils.

Herbaceous. A plant that is not woody (i.e., without stiff, woody stems).

Leach. To remove by the action of a percolating liquid; specifically, near the sea, to remove salt by rinsing or soaking with fresh water.

Lee. The side (as of a hillside) that is sheltered from the wind.

Native. A plant that is indigenous to a particular place.

Naturalized. In horticulture, a term applied to an exotic plant that has become established in a new setting. Ultimately, a naturalized plant reproduces and multiplies independently (without the assistance of a gardener).

Perennial. A plant that lasts for more than two growing seasons.

pH. A measure of acidity, used in testing soil. The pH scale runs from 1 to 14: 1 is extremely acidic, 7 is neutral, and 14 is extremely alkaline.

Retaining wall. A wall that supports soil on one side; a wall that is not freestanding and is specially designed to resist soil pressure.

Shelterbelt. A mixed planting designed to break the wind, typically consisting of several different types of trees and shrubs.

Transpiration. The evaporation of moisture from the leaves and stems of plants.

INDEX

Numbers in italics indicate illustrations.

A

Aaron's beard, 83
Acacia, 71
  blackwood, 70
  gossamer Syndey, 84
Abkhazi, Nicholas, *9*
Acton, Arthur, 74
Adam's needle, 66
Aeonium, *71,* 71
African daisy, 83
Agapanthus, 79
Agave, *71*
Allees, 75, *79,* 79
Aloe, 70
Alpine plants, 16
Althaea (hibiscus), 73, 75, 85
Alyssum, *59, 77*
  annual, 78
  perennial, 83
Amaryllis, 71
American beach grass, 47, 82
American Tree Care, 60
Amusement parks, 11
Anemone, 71
Annapolis, Md., 9
Annuals, 19, *24, 30,* 31, *54*
  lists, 73, 79, 82
Antidessicants, 60
Aralia, 71
Arctostaphylos Uva-ursi. See Bearberry
Army Corps of Engineers, 52
Aronia (chokeberry), 72
Artemisia, *53,* 54, 73
Artichoke, globe, 21
Asparagus fern, 76
Asphalt, 53
Aster, 19, *53,* 73
Astilbe, 73
Atlantic City, N.J., 11
Australian pine, *42,* 54, *74,* 75, 76, 86
Awnings, 38, 39
Australian tea tree, 85
Azalea. *See* Rhododendron

B

Baby's breath, 78, 79, 84
Bahamas, *12*
Banyan, 87
Bay, sweet, 73
Bayberry, 23, 29, 46, 72, 73, 77, 78, *79,* 85
Beach grass, 24, 31, 47
  American, 47, 78, 82
Beaches, gardens adjoining, 23
Beach pea, 45
Beach plum, 23, 29, 46, 78, *79,* 85
Beach strawberry, 83
Bearberry, *72, 73, 77,* 83
  cotoneaster, 77, 78, 83
Beech, 42, 87
Begonia, *56*
Bell, Mackenzie, *25*
Bellflower (campanula), *58,* 83
Benches, 67, 68, 77
Bermuda, *11*
Bermuda grass, 82
Birch, 79
Birds, 23
Bishop pine, 69, 70
Bittersweet, 88
Black-eyed Susan, 45
Blithewold Gardens and Arboretum, *40*
Bluebeard (caryopteris), 54, 66, 73, 84
Bluebell, *25, 49*
Blueberry, high-bush, 77, 78, 86
Boardwalks, 31, 53, *67,* 67–68, 77
Bone meal, 54
Botanical names, 55–56
Bottlebrush, 70
Bougainvillea, *12,* 31, 75, 76, 88
Boxwood, 9, 31, 35, *49,* 73
Bradford pear, 66
Breakers, Newport, *12*
Breakwaters, *34,* 76
Brick, 53, 67
Brighton Royal Pavilion, 10
British Columbia, *9*
British gardens, *9, 10,* 10, *17*
Bromeliads, 71
Broom, 66, 85
  Warminster, 78

Browallia, 73
Brussels sprouts, 21
Buckthorn, 85
Buildings as shelter, 34
Bulbs, 31, 71
Butterfly bush, 70, 84
Buttonwood, 75, 76
Bye, A.E., 13, 23

C

Cabbage, 21
Cabbage tree, 70, 86
Calcium, 19
California poppy, 82
Camellia, 19, 70, 84
Campanula (bellflower), *58,* 83
Candytuft, 79, 83
Cape honeysuckle, 88
Carpobrotus (Hottentot fig), *23,* 83
Caryopteris (bluebeard), *54,* 66, 73, 84
Cassia, 71
Catalpa, 86
Catbrier, 88
Ceanothus (California lilac), *43,* 84
Cedar, 86
  Japanese, 86
  red, 29, 44, 45, 78, 87
Centipede grass, 68, 82
Century plant (agave), 71
Chalfin, 74
Champlain, Samuel de, 10
Cherry, 87
Chicory, 45
Chokeberry (aronia), 72
Chrysanthemum, *58,* 83
Cineraria, 71
  annual (dusty-miller), 29, 45, *56,* 82, 83
Cinquefoil, 73, 85
Classical gardens, 75
Clematis, 45, 72, 88
  wild, 39
Cleome (spider flower), *77,* 78, 82
Clethra (summersweet), 72, 77, 78, 84
Cliff green, 73, 83
Coastal Zone Management Act, 52
Cobbles, 53